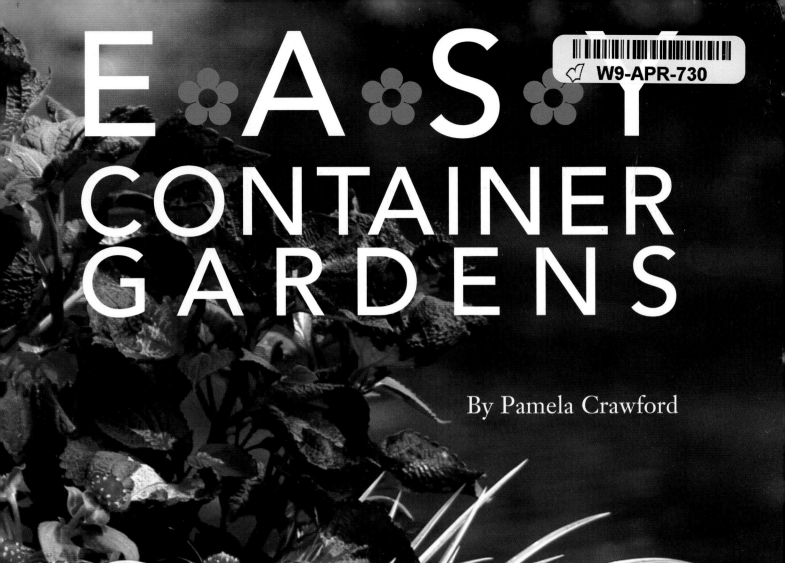

EASY

CONTAINER
GARDENS

By Pamela Crawford

Where to Buy "Easy Container Gardens" Book:

The book is available through many garden centers and book sellers. It is also available through www.kinsmangarden.com and www.amazon.com. To locate your nearest source or place an order with the publisher, contact us at:

Color Garden Publishing
1353 Riverstone Parkway, Canton, GA 30114
Phone: 770-704-6437   Fax: 770-720-9719
Web site: www.easygardencolor.com
Email: info@easygardencolor.com

Credits:

Author: Pamela Crawford
Research Assistant: Barbara Hadsell
Cover Design and Graphic Design Assistance: Elaine Weber Designs, Inc. (www.ewdlogos.com)
Proofreader: Barbara Iderosa, Best Editing Service, Wellington, Florida
Landscape Design: Pamela Crawford
Photography: All photos by Pamela Crawford except for the following:
      Page 53, Kinsman Corp.
      Scaevola photos on page 17, 35, 116, 132, and 161; New Guinea
      impatiens on pages 92 and 94; Euphorbia 'Diamond Frost' on pages
      106 and 167; Schizanthus on page 169; Dicondra 'Silver Falls' on
      pages 16, 107, 127, and 150 from Proven Winners;
      Pages 6-7 and pages 42-43: Marvin Cargle.
Printing: Asianprinting.com, Korea

Published by Color Garden, Inc., Canton, GA. First printing: 2008. Second printing: 2008. Third printing: 2009.

Library of Congress Catalog Card Number pending

ISBN 10: 0-9712220-6-1
ISBN 13: 978-0-9712220-6-9

Cover photo from Gibbs Gardens in Ball Ground, Georgia. Complete profile on pages 100-101.

Right: Canna lilies surrounded by dragon wing begonias.

Contents

Book Background

When people ask me what I do, I tell them that I write gardening books. Most people tell me that they routinely kill plants. I am writing this book for them.

This book deals with easy container gardening, which is a joy to write about. The new potting mixes and fertilizers have simplified container gardening like never before, and most people are not yet aware of this. It is now commonplace to plant a container in spring and have it last for a full six or seven month growing period.

It is difficult for many people to figure out which plants last all season. Gerber daisies, which only bloom for about a month, are displayed right next to wax begonias, which bloom at least six months. Most plant labels don't say how long the plant blooms. I bought Gerber daisies when I first started gardening and was quite disappointed when they just bloomed for a month, thinking I was a terrible gardener. That was not the case - gerber daisies are only supposed to bloom for a month! If I had this book with me at the garden center, I never would have bought them.

My gardening failures continued for many years, and I know only too well the frustration of killing plants or not having them live up to my expectations. These early errors started a three-decade saga of learning everything I could about gardening, especially how to make gardening easier. After receiving a master's degree in landscape architecture, I then started a nursery and garden design business. While designing 1500 gardens, I also started my own trial gardens (on the eight acres where I lived and worked) to determine which plants gave the best performances with the least amount of care.

During my first 10 years of having my own trial gardens, I tried 2500 landscape plants and killed 2300. I have spent the last four years trialing container plants, planting about 10,000 and killing only about 300. Obviously, container gardening is a lot easier than landscape gardening! So, I want to tell the world!

It is easy to plant a container with good potting mix, state-of-the-art fertilizer, and great plants. Then, for the rest of the container garden's life, all it needs is water! That's it! Most people are unaware of this, and I think we would greatly increase the numbers of people planting containers if they only knew how easy it could be.

I hope this book gets that word out, so all the other plant killers can turn into great gardeners quickly, joyfully, and easily!

Thank You

Barbara Hadsell

Elaine Golob Weber

I want to thank Barbara Hadsell, my assistant. Barbara tested the plants in New Hampshire, Georgia and Florida. She also gave lots of ideas for our Georgia trial garden, and tirelessly worked with me in 100 degree and higher temperatures. In addition, Barbara gave lectures and workshops on container gardening and set up trade shows to spread the word of our latest ideas. She is consistently energetic, smart, and tireless!

Michele Kinsman

Graham Kinsman

Marvin Cargle helps with planting, maintenance, photography, and videos.

Graham Kinsman and his wife, Michele, worked tirelessly with me for over two years to develop the side planted baskets shown in Chapter 6.

Elaine Weber, the graphic designer, worked enthusiastically with me on some very tight deadlines. She showed great patience with my last-minute requests.

USDA Plant Hardiness Map

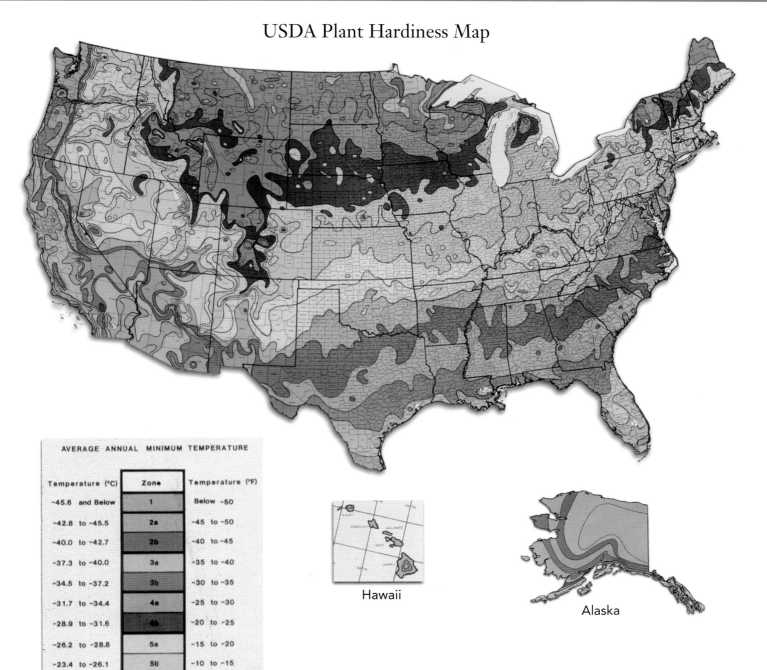

Hawaii

Alaska

AVERAGE ANNUAL MINIMUM TEMPERATURE		
Temperature (°C)	Zone	Temperature (°F)
-45.6 and Below	1	Below -50
-42.8 to -45.5	2a	-45 to -50
-40.0 to -42.7	2b	-40 to -45
-37.3 to -40.0	3a	-35 to -40
-34.5 to -37.2	3b	-30 to -35
-31.7 to -34.4	4a	-25 to -30
-28.9 to -31.6	4b	-20 to -25
-26.2 to -28.8	5a	-15 to -20
-23.4 to -26.1	5b	-10 to -15
-20.6 to -23.3	6a	-5 to -10
-17.8 to -20.5	6b	0 to -5
-15.0 to -17.7	7a	5 to 0
-12.3 to -15.0	7b	10 to 5
-9.5 to -12.2	8a	15 to 10
-6.7 to -9.4	8b	20 to 15
-3.9 to -6.6	9a	25 to 20
-1.2 to -3.8	9b	30 to 25
1.6 to -1.1	10a	35 to 30
4.4 to 1.7	10b	40 to 35
4.5 and Above	11	40 and Above

The country is divided into zones based on minimum temperatures. Plants are classified by these zone numbers to determine where they can grow based on the lowest temperature they can take.

USDA Miscellaneous Publication No. 1475. Issued January 1990. Authored by Henry M. Cathey while Director, U.S. National Arboretum.

Edited, formatted and prepared for the US National Arboretum web site by Ramon Jordan, March 1998 & Revised March 2001 U.S. National Arboretum, Agricultural Research Service, U.S. Department of Agriculture, Washington, DC 20002 Special thanks to Jody Stuart and Scott Bauer, ARS Information Staff

Chapter 1

Easy Basics

Skim this chapter before planting your first container. It will save you a lot of time, money, and trouble – and make container gardening a lot easier for you.

I have planted tens of thousands of plants in containers in order to find out what's easy and what's not. This chapter tells the story.

See this chapter for easy instructions on these key areas:

✿ Seven easy ways to kill plants

✿ Differences between container gardens and gardens planted in the ground.

✿ Easiest plants for container gardens

✿ Regional differences

✿ Easy container design

✿ Easy planting techniques

✿ Reduction in the need to water

✿ Assessing light conditions

✿ Easy planting and maintenance

Seven Easy Ways to Kill Plants

1. Buy the Wrong Plants

These calatheas are gorgeous but only bloom for a short time.

Most beginners buy plants that don't meet their expectations simply because they don't understand the plant's flowering habits - or that the plant is an erratic performer.

Take this book with you to your garden center. If you stick to the blue ribbon plants described on pages eight to eleven (and shown in chapter 9), you will have a great chance of success with tough plants that bloom for all or most of your growing season.

See pages 20-24 for tips on how to buy other plants at your local garden center.

2. Buy the Wrong Potting Mix

Don't skimp on your potting mix. Good potting mix costs a little bit more but makes all the difference. The plants grow larger and live longer with quality potting mix. ***Do not buy topsoil, garden soil, or potting soil for containers. It is too heavy, and the plants may rot and die quickly.***

Look for a brand name you trust. Peters, Miracle Grow, Lambert's and Fafard (along with many others) offer top-quality potting mix.

3. Buy the Wrong Fertilizer

I have killed plants by using fertilizers several times. My first lawn died from over fertilization. Years later, an entire garden my landscaping company planted died because the popular, slow-release fertilizer we used released all three month's worth of nutrients at once. Water causes the fertilizer to activate, and we had a lot of rain. I don't want to kill plants because of such a routine occurrence!

So, I kept using new products. A fertilizer salesman gave me some samples of a new fertilizer that was supposed to be perfect for the flowers I was growing in my nursery. Luckily, I had the sense to test it on about 25 plants before I tried it on thousands. All 25 plants were dead within a week!

Liquid fertilizers (the blue powder you mix with water in a hose sprayer and spray on your plants) is supposed to be the mildest product on the market. A good friend of mine burned up about half her garden with that product.

But, there is good news! I finally found a product made that not only didn't kill my plants but also made them look like a magazine cover, I got so excited about it that I put my name on it. See more about fertilizer on page 46.

4. Water Incorrectly

Like people, plants need water to live. However, if you give plants too much, they die from drowning. If you give them too little, they die of thirst.

Luckily, knowing when and how much to water is quite easy. See pages 48-51 for this information.

5. Pile Potting Mix Around the Stem of the Plant

If potting mix or organic mulch comes into contact with the stem of many plants, the stem rots, killing the plant. It is quite easy to avoid this plight by simply planting the plants a little higher, as shown in the drawing.

To help retain water, some people like to put organic mulch on top of the potting mix after they have planted a container. This method works fine on large plants, like azaleas or ti plants, provided you don't pile the mulch up around the stem. However, on small annuals, like impatiens, it is quite difficult to mulch without harming the plant.

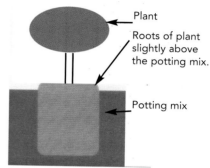

Plant

Roots of plant slightly above the potting mix.

Potting mix

Proper planting method: Roots can be slightly above the potting mix to avoid stem rot.

6. Plant in a Pot Without Holes in the Bottom

If your pots don't have holes in the bottom for drainage, the plants will die (unless the pot is specially designed for self watering). See page 38 to learn how to drill holes in the bottoms of pots.

Luckily, most pots come with holes in the bottom. If you see one you want to buy that doesn't have holes, ask the salesperson if she will drill them for you. Many garden centers offer that service.

7. Plant in the Wrong Amount of Light

Different plants need different amounts of light. A petunia (shown) likes sun, while a dieffenbachia likes shade. But how much sun is enough for sun plants? The rule of thumb is at least four to six hours of direct sun a day. In other words, if your petunia just gets two hours of sun with shade the rest of the day, it will not do well.

For your shade-only plants, if they are left in the sun, the leaves and flowers will burn. Of the two, shade plants are more complicated to place than sun plants. See pages 34-35 for more information on shade gardening.

Container Gardens are Different from

Container Gardens are Easier than Landscape Gardens

It is easier for plants to survive in containers than in the ground, which makes container gardening ideal for beginning gardeners. Since decorative container gardens are normally used for one season, you don't have to worry about long term plant success, which is more difficult. And, they are much easier to plant in containers than digging in your yard!

I tried planting succulents in the ground, and they rotted after we had a lot of rain (18" from a tropical storm). In containers they thrived with the same rain. The containers allowed the plants to drain easier (photo from Thomas Hobbs residence in Vancouver).

You also don't have to worry about your native soil if you use the great potting mix I recommend on page 8.

Container Gardens are Fast and Instant

For many years, I owned a landscaping business that renovated home landscapes. I was used to huge projects that took months to complete.

I get a tremendous feeling of accomplishment by finishing a container garden so quickly. I photographed this one shortly after planting.

The plants include *Philodendron* 'Kaleidascope', moss fern, fuschia 'Autumale', coleus, fiber optic grass, and dieffenbachia. The pots are Campania's *Adige Ovals* in Garda Green. Look for them at www.campaniainternational.com.

Planting in the Ground

Container Plants need More Water Than Plants in the Ground

Plants need more water in containers because their roots (which store water) can't grow beyond the limits of the pot. However, with the latest automatic watering systems, this chore does not require anywhere near as much time as in years past. See pages 48-51 for ideas on easy watering.

Plant Closer Together in Containers

This was a hard one for me to get used to. After years of landscaping, I was accustomed to spacing plants so they had room to grow. It is imperative that shrubs, trees, and perennials have enough space to grow appropriately, or they won't thrive.

Decorative container gardens are just the opposite; they are designed for seasonal display. The plants need to be planted quite close together in order to provide a finished product quickly. And it works! I was worried that close planting would kill the plants, but they have thrived!

This container, planted with a copperleaf centerpiece and pilea side plants, was photographed shortly after planting. The plants are planted quite close together.. The container is Anamese's *Beehive*, medium (15"W x 15"H) in copper. Look for it on www.anamese.com.

Plants Can't Live Forever in the Same Pot

In nature, plant roots grow as much as they want. The top of the plant grows proportionally - it gets larger as the roots grow. If the roots reach a barrier - like the edges of a pot - the plant stops growing. Eventually, the roots fill the pot and the plant goes into a decline.

Nurseries start seedlings in tiny pots and move them into larger ones as the plants grow. If you are keeping plants for a long period, you should do the same.

Some plants can stay in the same pot longer than others, including bromeliads, crotons, and succulents. The bromeliads, shown left, can stay in that size container for up to two years. The center plant will only flower for about three months a year, however.

Plants last longer in larger containers, as shown on pages 24-25.

Our Plant Trials

In the First Ten Years of Landscape Trials, 2300 Plants Died

As a gardener, I initially had more bad luck than good. Many of my plants died because of one blunder after another. But, I just loved flowers, and this led me to pursue a career in the landscaping business. I received a master's degree in landscape architecture, which included a master's thesis in plants that were well adapted to the environment (or easy plants).

Shortly after graduation, I started a nursery so I could grow plants for my landscaping customers. I moved into a house on the nursery grounds and quickly started my dream - large trial gardens that would mimic the average yard. For the first five years, I had no automatic watering system - the plants got water once a week if it didn't rain. None of them were sprayed with pesticides. I trimmed them once a year, at the most. None of them were pampered in the least.

At the end of ten years, 2500 different plants had been planted in my gardens. Of them, 2300 were dead. Many would look upon this low survival rate as a complete failure. I looked upon it as a wonderful success because I had 200 great plants!

I then wrote two books about landscape plants before beginning to research plants for container gardens.

Container Trials Yield More Success

I traveled all over the US and into Canada to begin research on container gardens. It was quite exciting to see the new plants and containers in so many varying areas. It was also quite enlightening to learn how similar container gardens were - even in areas with quite different climates.

After getting home, I decided to test what I had seen, so I would be able to write about the easiest plants and combinations. I planted thousands of plants in hundreds of different containers, so I could learn the best of the best. By doing it myself, I was able to watch each container combination to see exactly how long it lasted as well as what type of maintenance it required to keep it looking its best.

Luckily, many more plants thrived in my container trials than in my landscape trials. Also, the regional differences were much fewer, so I was able to learn about plants that did well in most areas of the world.

I became fascinated with container gardens. This is my third book on the subject, and I am just getting started!

All of these photos are of my original trial gardens. These gardens led me to holding the world's record in plant homicide but also taught me about some really easy plants!

Blue Ribbon Plants are the Easiest

1ST

The easiest, blue ribbon container plants require nothing but water if you follow the planting and fertilization instructions in this chapter! That's right - just plant them, add water as needed, and do absolutely nothing else for the full lifespan of the container! Although I show other plants in the container profiles of this book, I recommend that beginners or serial plant killers stick to the blue ribbon plants until they have some successful growing experiences.

Above: Begonias are one of the most useful blue ribbon plants.

Characteristics of the Blue Ribbon Plant

❀ Dependable. Performs the same way every year

❀ Requires little to no trimming

❀ Adjusts to most climates

❀ Lives a long life - at least the four to six months of your growing season

❀ Fares well with little pest susceptibility

❀ Established record - it's been around for enough years to fully understand it.

❀ Blooms continuously for a minimum of five to six months (except for cacti, bromeliads and plants used primarily for leaf color).

It takes many years on the market for a plant to be a reliable success. Plants that require little water are wonderful to work with. Unfortunately, there are not many that can survive long in containers without water. Cacti and succulents are the exceptions and are rapidly gaining popularity. See Chapter 7, pages 134-141 for great ideas with succulents.

Right: White caladiums, wax begonias, and ivy are three blue ribbon plants combined in one container. This arrangement's only need is water for its entire lifespan - if planted and fertilized as instructed in this chapter.

Blue Ribbon Arrangements Have it All!

The blue ribbon arrangement is planted with blue ribbon plants and:

❀ Follows the planting specifications given on pages 44-45.

❀ Is planted in containers that are large enough to sustain the plants for a five to six month growing season.

So, you don't have to touch them - other than water - after planting! And if you don't like the watering chore, see pages 50-51 for some ideas on cutting back on water. If you hook them up to a drip irrigation system (pretty easy to do), you don't have to touch them at all!

1ST

Best Use: C = Centerpiece   E = Edge Plant

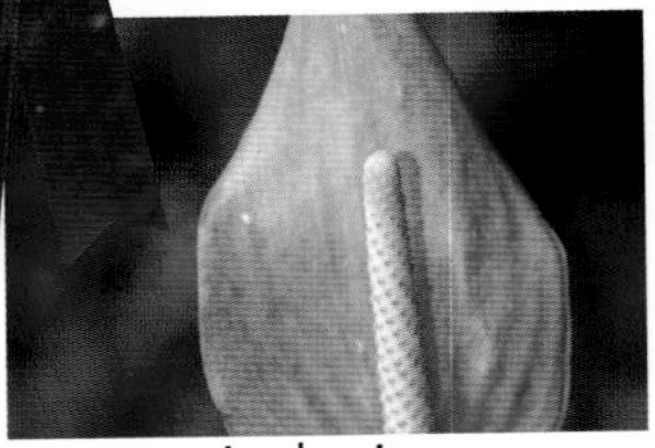

Anthurium
C

Begonia, Dragon Wing
C or E

Begonia, Wax
E

Bromeliad
C or E

Cabbage, Ornamental
E

Cacti
E

Caladium
C or E

Chenille Plant
C

Chenille Plant, Dwarf*
E

Creeping Jenny*
E

Croton
C or E

Daisy, California Bush
C or E

Dicondra 'Silver Falls'*
E

Dieffenbachia
C

Diplademia
C

Dracaena
C

Elephant Ear
C

Fern
C or E

Grasses
C or E

Impatiens, Double
C or E

Impatiens, Regular
C or E

Ivy*
E

Jatropha
C

Lamium*
E

Just Add Water!

Licorice Plant, Silver
E

Lysimachia 'Outback Sunset'   E

Melampodium
C or E

Mint, Variegated*
E

Pansy
E

Persian Shield
E

Phormium or Flax
C

Pothos*
E

Purple Queen
E

Salvia, Annual
C or E

Scaevola*
E

Sedum
E

Shrimp Plant, Golden
C or E

Succulents
C or E

Syngonium or Nephthytis
E

Ti Plant
C

Torenia, Trailing
E

Vinca Illumination*
E

Vinca Vine*
E

Viola
E

This trailing plant may require a hair cut if it trails so long that it touches the ground.

Red Ribbon Plants

Red Ribbon Plants

Red ribbon plants are not far behind the blue ribbon plants in overall performance. The only differences are that red ribbon plants either have some susceptibility to pests or require trimming or grooming every month or so.

Coleus (along with perilla), for example, is one of the most popular container plants. However, it requires pinching every month or so; thus it didn't make the cut into the blue ribbon category. New Guinea impatiens have been one of the easiest plants in my trials but are sometimes troubled by fungal problems or Japanese beetles. Geraniums are another of the world's most popular container plants, but they look much better if you remove the dead flowers, which places them in the red ribbon category.

Canna lilies are very easy to grow but are frequently attacked by snails or Japanese beetles. I grow them anyway and put up with a few holes in the leaves.

The photos shown right show the red ribbon plants you are most likely to find at your local garden center. See Chapter 8 for all of them.

Red Ribbon Arrangements

Red ribbon arrangements are planted with red ribbon plants and:

❀ Follow the planting specifications given on pages 44-45.

❀ Planted in containers that are large enough to sustain the plants for a five to six month growing season.

The container combination on the left consists of two red ribbon plants, perilla (the tall plant) and trailing geraniums (in front). The container on the right repeats the trailing geraniums but includes a coleus as a centerpiece. All three plants are quite easy to grow but require pinching or removal of dead flowers to keep them looking good. This needed maintenance kept them from the blue ribbon category. Both arrangements are planted in containers large enough to sustain the plants through a six month growing season.

Occasional Trimming and Pests

Red Ribbon Plants (Best Use: C = Centerpiece   E = Edge Plant)

Canna Lily
Profile: Page 147

Coleus
Profile: Page 148

Geranium
Profile: Page 152

Impatiens, New Guinea
Profile: Page 154

Perilla
Profile: Page 159

Characteristics of the Red Ribbon Plant

❀ Dependable. Performs the same way every year.

❀ Adjusts well to most climates

❀ Requires trimming every month or so

❀ Has a long lifespan, at least the four to six months of your growing season

❀ May have some susceptibility to pests

❀ Established record (that takes many years on the market for a plant to be a reliable success).

❀ Blooms continuously for a minimum of five to six months (except for cacti and bromeliads or plants used primarily for leaf color.)

Plants that require little water are wonderful to work with. Unfortunately, there are not many that can survive long in containers without much water. Cacti and succulents are the exceptions and are rapidly gaining popularity. See Chapter 7, pages 136-141 for some great ideas with succulents.

Take this book with you when you go to garden centers. When you see a plant you need information on, check the index to find the appropriate pages.

This book is limited to plants that are great for containers, so don't expect to see shade trees and evergreen shrubs within its pages. Most container plants are annuals and live only one season. Annuals usually have a much higher percentage of color than long-blooming perennials. Since the purpose of container gardens is largely decorative, annuals are usually the best choice.

I also list plants in the last chapter that are commonly available but might not meet your expectations. That information can save you a lot of time, frustration, and money.

Some Plants Might not Meet Your Expectations

I purchased these lovely gerber daisies (top photo), thinking they would bloom throughout my growing season, or at least six months or so. Not so. They bloomed for a month and never even set another bud. I thought I had done something wrong until I found out that gerber daisies are supposed to only bloom for a month. Had I known that, I would have bought one plant instead of the six I planted in this pot for $4 each!

But the label didn't say how long the plant bloomed, and the garden center lady told me she thought they bloomed for months. She was wrong.

I had the same experience with the kalanchoe (bottom photo). It looked great the day I planted it but only stayed in bloom for about a month.

Many garden center personnel are encyclopedias of plant knowledge. Others are novices in gardening.

The hardest information to find is how long the plant blooms. So take this book with you. The plant you are looking for may not be here, but chances are it will.

If you see a plant you like that is not in this book, by all means ask the garden center personnel. Be sure to ask if they have any personal experience with the plant.

Plants You See in Garden Centers?

Great Plants That are Hit or Miss

One of my favorite container plants is petunias. I tried eight different varieties of trailing petunias this past season, and they all did beautifully. I've had great luck with some of the Wave petunias from Pan American Seed as well as the Supertunias from Proven Winners (shown left, at one of their growing facilities in Vancouver).

So, why aren't they blue ribbon plants? Several reasons:

❀ Many petunias sold today are unnamed. The label just says 'Petunia.' Quite a few of these died on me. I'm afraid if I class them as the best of the best, you might end up with one of these bad ones and be quite disappointed.

The blue ribbon plants are also sold as unnamed plants, but the species are so strong that all of them do well. Wax begonias and impatiens are both examples of this - they are almost foolproof - named or unnamed.

❀ One of the most important criteria for blue ribbon plants is at least a four to six month lifespan. Most petunias won't last that long, particularly if the weather is quite hot.

However, I do show petunias in the container profiles in this book because the good ones are soooo good!

Erratic Performers

Calibrachoa, or million bells, is one of the hottest and prettiest plants in container gardening. However, when they are good, they are very, very good; and when they are bad, they are awful!

I'm not sure why. Probably, some of the new ones haven't been tried in certain climates and might not like it there. Eventually, they will sort themselves out.

I frequently use calibrachoa because I really like the plant. Sometimes, it is fantastic, other times not.

Once again, take this book with you to your garden center so you will have a better shot at assessing your risk with certain plants. In many instances, they are so inexpensive that cost is not an issue. However, it is important that both new gardeners and serial plant killers have successful gardening experiences. So, stick with the blue ribbon plants if you fall into either of those categories.

Regional Differences

Container plants are much more adaptable than landscape plants are to different climates. Since container plants are are used primariy in spring, summer, and fall, they don't have winter temperatures to contend with. And, since you use potting mix instead of native soils, you have knocked out another regional issue.

Extreme heat can be a problem. I experienced it last summer for the first time - we had ten days straight with temperatures over 100 degrees. I thought all my beautiful containers would cook! They drove me crazy with water needs but survived quite well. Next summer, I'll have a drip watering system - see pages 48-51 for more information. All of the plants in the containers were supposed to take a lot of heat, and they did. Many of them are in this book.

My adult life has been spent in Houston (a short stint), south Florida (a long time) and north Georgia. We tried most of the plants in this book in Florida as well as in New Hampshire, where my assistant, Barbara Hadsell, spent her summers.

In preparation for my first book on container gardening (this is my third), I traveled all over the country to see how container gardening differed in different areas. I was quite surprised to see the similarities. I saw the same plants in New York and Chicago that I was used to seeing in the south.

Cool summers make gardening easier than hot weather. I envy so many coastal Californians who seldom see temperatures go above 90 degrees. They have much more variety to choose from, and I haven't tested anywhere near as many plants as they have to choose from.

Most of my blue and red ribbon plants grow throughout the world and represent the most dependable plants available in most areas, where the temperatures get into the low to mid 90's for a lot of the summer. I also had experience with cool weather plants during my years in south Florida, where the winters are the primary growing season. Our winter high temperatures averaged in the mid 70's to low 80's.

In containers, I have grown thousands of plants from all over the world. And I still have millions to go! The sheer quantity of plants that are currently on the market is what makes my job so exciting. If you come across one you don't see in this book but it appeals to you, please let me know at info@easygardencolor.com. I hope my experiences help you kill fewer plants than you did before!

Left: These three containers all feature blue ribbon plants in different geographic areas. Top: Succulents at Landcraft Environment, Long Island, New York. Middle: Elephant ear underplanted with geraniums, wax begonias, and vincas in downtown Vancouver, Canada. Bottom: Succulents at The Butchart Gardens Ltd., Victoria, BC, Canada.

Right: My trial gardens in Florida

Plants Last Longer in Large Containers

Plants in larger containers are easier to care for than those in smaller ones. The plants live longer because their roots have more room to spread. And they require less water because there is more room for water storage. The mixed flowers (below) have a shorter lifespan and require more frequent waterings than the mixed flowers in the larger container, right.

Below: The white bowl includes hot pink pentas as a centerpiece, surrounded by yellow and pink coleus and blue torenia. The bright colored containers (from www.masart.com) include red geraniums, blue salvia, and orange gallardia.

Right: Plantings include Mona lavender for the centerpiece surrounded by yellow gaillardia and red petunias. The container is a full 20 inches wide (inside diameter).

Simple Plants in Great Pots

This simple diffenbachia looks good because it is planted in a spectacular pot. Follow these guidelines for great results:

❀ Putting one plant in a non-descript pot doesn't work - it looks blah.

❀ Use great pots for single plantings.

❀ A great pot makes a design statement either by its overall design or its scale. Simple pots that are oversized have much more impact than the same design in a much smaller size, as shown in the photo to the right. This pot (planted with a croton) is a full three feet tall. It looks great even when empty!

❀ Large pots are easier because they require less water.

❀ Container gardens planted in large pots last longer than those in smaller ones.

The gold glaze on this column is absolutely gorgeous! For more information about this pot series, see pages 64-65.

Use Centerpieces for Mixed Plantings

Plant the tallest plant in the middle and smaller ones around it. What could be easier! We call the big plant the centerpiece.

Characteristics of Good Centerpieces

❀ A centerpiece can be any type of plant as long as it remains taller than the surrounding plants for the life of the arrangement. See pages 16-17 for photos of blue ribbon centerpieces.

❀ Choose a plant that is full, or combine several tall, skinny plants together so the centerpiece doesn't look too skinny.

❀ Be sure the centerpiece likes the same growing conditions (light, temperature, water) as the smaller plants that go around it.

Above: Pink pentas form the centerpiece surrounded by blue upright torenia.

Right: A golden shrimp plant forms the centerpiece with a hot pink penta in front of it. Blue trailing torenia is planted along the front edge.

Mix Textures for Easy Success

Spiky Plants

Spiky plants have long, narrow, upright leaves. Pop one in the middle of a pot, and surround it with both mounding and trailing plants, and you have instant success!

This grass is called rush, or *Juncus* grass. I have had many great successes with it.

Some other easy spiky plants include bromeliads, many other grasses, phormium (flax), dracaenas, and ti plants. Salvia are also considered spiky because their flowers are tall and narrow, like a spike.

Mounding Plants

Mounding plants grow in a neat, mound-like shape, like the New Guinea impatiens shown here.

Some other mounding plants include begonias, ornamental cabbages, caladiums, crotons, impatiens, pansies, upright torenia, and violas.

Trailing Plants

Trailing plants trail down the sides of the container, like the creeping Jenny (left).

Some other easy trailing plants include ivy, scaevola, trailing torenia, and vinca vine.

Right: This combination is an excellent example of an easy container garden. I planted it in April and enjoyed it until October. The impatiens bloomed the entire time. Other than watering, I only had to trim the creeping Jenny twice to keep it from spreading all over the deck.

Spiky plus Mounding and Trailing

Combine the Three for Easy Success

Centerpieces with Large Leaves

This is one of the easiest design ideas I know for major, quick impact. Just plant a plant with large leaves in the middle of the pot, and surround it with ANY smaller plant that has smaller leaves. That's it! Instant impact.

Great plants with large leaves include elephant ears, bananas, canna lilies, and diffenbachia.

Above: Canna lilies with yellow leaves look great with a mixture of mounding and trailing plants. Photo from Minter Gardens in Chilliwack, BC, Canada.

Right: The elephant ear centerpiece makes such a strong design statement that it works well with simple underplantings, like these dragon wing begonias and creeping Jenny.

Easy Recipe for Success

Understand Light

Different plants need different amounts of light. A petunia likes sun, while a dieffenbachia likes shade. But how much sun is enough for sun plants? The rule of thumb is at least four to six hours of direct sun per day for sun plants. In other words, if your petunia just gets two hours of sun with shade the rest of the day, it will not do well.

If you put a plant that just likes shade in the sun, the leaves and flowers will burn. And, shade is more complicated than sun. It's pretty easy to tell whether your area is in sun; but, shade is trickier. Many plants are quite sensitive to varying degrees of shade - light, medium, and dense. Sit in the same location you are considering for a container and look around.

Light Shade

Look up, and you will see about 20-30% leaves and the rest sky. The trees are planted farther apart in light shade than in medium shade. Look down, and notice many types of plants growing. Look around, and see many patches of sky from any direction.

Plants that grow well in light shade also thrive in part-sun, part-shade situations - provided the sun is in the morning hours. If your area gets sun all afternoon, choose plants that tolerate full sun.

Medium Shade

Look up, and you will see medium shade from trees. Look for about 50% or more of sky. Look down, and see ferns or other shade plants growing. Look around, and see more trees but not much open sky on the south or west sides. Sun from the south or west is strong and too much for most medium shade plants.

Fewer plants grow in medium shade than dense shade, but your choices are still wide enough to make a great, colorful container.

Dense Shade

Look up, and you will see the dense shade of very thick trees or the roof of a building. Less than 30% of the sky is visible. Look down and see almost nothing growing, except possibly a few weeds. Look all around, and you will still see very little sky but rather more thickly-leafed trees or buildings.

Many plants thrive in light to medium shade. Dense shade, however, is a difficult situation. Most flowering plants require more light than dense shade provides. Stick to plants you find in the house plant section of your garden center for dense shade situations.

Popular Blue and Red Ribbon Plants Organized by Light Needs

S = Full sun   L = Light shade   M = Medium shade   D = Dense shade

Begonia, Dragon Wing* L, M	Begonia, Wax S, L, M	Bromeliads** S, L, M	Cabbage S, L	Cactus** S, L, M
Caladium** L, M	Canna Lily S, L, M	Coleus S, L, M	Creeping Jenny S, L, M	Croton S, L, M
Dieffenbachia L, M, D	Dracaena L, M, D	Elephant Ears S, L, M	Geraniums S, L	Grasses** S, L, M
Impatiens* L, M	Impatiens, Double* L, M	Impatiens, New Guinea* L, M	Ivy L, M, D	Licorice Plant, Silver S, L
Melampodium S, L, M	Mint, Variegated S, L, M	Pansy S, L, M	Perilla S, L, M	Persian Shield S, L, M
Phormium or Flax S, L, M	Salvia, Annual S, L	Scaevola S, L	Sedum S, L	Shrimp Plant S, L, M
Succulents** S, L, M	Ti Plant S, L, M	Torenia S, L	Vinca Vine S, L, M	Viola S, L, M

* Takes sun only in short, cool days - like winters in south Florida - not the average summer.
**Light tolerance depends on type, e.g. some varieties take full sun while others don't.

Plants That Don't Drop Much

Many plants drop flowers that are a pain in the neck to get off patios. Impatiens are one of the worst. Most, but not all, flowers stick to hard surfaces, making them difficult to sweep away. Leaf color is ideal for patio areas, like the grasses and coleus shown below.

Ideal for Patios and Pool areas

Easy Plants That don't Shed Much

Bromeliad
Profile: Page 146

Cabbage, Ornamental
Profile: Page 146

Cacti
Profile: Page 147

Caladium
Profile: Page 147

Canna lily
Profile: Page 147

Coleus
Profile: Page 148

Creeping Jenny
Profile: Page 149

Crotons
Profile: Page 149

Dieffenbachia
Profile: Page 150

Elephant Ears
Profile: Page 152

Grasses
Profile: Page 152-154

Ivy
Profile: Page 155

Licorice Plant, Silver
Profile: Page 156

Mint, Variegated
Profile: Page 158

Perilla
Profile: Page 159

Persian Shield
Profile: Page 159

Phormium
Profile: Page 160

Shrimp Plant
Profile: Page 162

Succulents
Profile: See index

Ti Plant
Profile: Page 164

Easy Pots

Be Sure Your Pot has a Hole in the Bottom

If your pot doesn't have holes in the bottom, the plants will die quickly - unless it's one of the self-watering containers, which will be marked as such. Most pots you buy already have holes in them.

What if yours doesn't? The white bowl in this photo had no holes when I bought it. I simply put a towel on a table (to protect the rim of the pot from chipping), turned the pot upside down on the towel, and drilled two holes in the bottom. Holes about 1/3" to 1/2" wide are fine.

I took my pot to the home improvement store first, so they could show me which drill bit to use. This glazed clay pot required a masonry drill bit.

In years past, you had to put a coffee filter, pot shards, or gravel on the bottom of the pot to keep the potting mix from escaping through the holes in the bottom. No need now. The new potting mixes don't run out through the bottom hole unless it is HUGE!

Aluminum

Aluminum is the only metal I tried that was really easy, unless you like the look of rust. I do, to an extent, and loved the iron pots shown on pages 62-63 and 92-93. They are supposed to rust.

Other iron pots I tried were not supposed to rust. Either they rusted in a few days (literally) or had to be recoated with a anti-rust material that was a pain in the neck to apply.

Aluminum is completely trouble free. I had the one shown left outdoors in Florida's tough climate for years, and it still looked the same as the day I bought it.

Fiberglass

Fiberglass is a great material for easy containers. It is lightweight, looks great, and cleans easily. Even experts could not tell fiberglass (made to look like cast stone or metal) from the real thing in my trial gardens.

Fiberglass lasts a long time - probably as long as you will! Good, quality fiberglass is not cheap, but it is worth every penny.

Clay Pots with Ceramic Glazes

Ceramic glazes have revolutionized the use of color on pots. I use them throughout this book in many different colors. They hold up well in the toughest of climates, although some of them have to be moved inside during freezes. Ask your supplier for more information.

Glazed pots are very low maintenance - they seldom require cleaning, and when they do, it's fairly easy. And they last for years. I have some that are ten years old and still look brand new.

The only disadvantage (unless you live in a windy area) is that they are quite heavy.

Some glazed pots take freezes and some don't. Ask your garden center experts about any pots you are considering for purchase.

Cast Stone Pots

Cast stone pots are made from a mold filled with concrete. The poured concrete ages gracefully as it cures. They come in a variety of finishes - like antique, moss, and patina. These finishes give the look of antique containers at a fraction of the cost.

They look great, last forever, and require little care. However, they are extremely heavy and don't tolerate freezes.

Terra Cotta

Terra cotta is one of the oldest and most common pot materials. If you like the look of the pot shown here, terra cotta is for you.

It looks orange when it is new, like clay. However, it requires cleaning to keep it that way. The cleaning process for terra cotta is much more difficult than the other pot types shown. If left alone, it molds like this pot has. This look is prized by some but not by others.

Side-Planted Containers

Step 1: Add soil up to the first hole. Wet the root balls of the plants, and squeeze them. Slide the root balls through the holes.

Step 2: Plant the centerpiece.

Step 3: Plant the edge plants.

Before

After - Just One Week After Planting!

Pots with Holes in Them!

Side-planted containers have holes in the sides that allow you to plant into the sides as well as the top for an instant look.

They are nothing short of spectacular! Look for hanging baskets, window boxes, and wall pots - plus spectacular baskets supported on column kits, as shown below.

These containers not only look great when planted but also stand the test of time. See Chapter 6 for many examples from my garden that looked great on planting day and lasted a full seven months - with a ten day run of temperatures over 100 degrees! See www.sideplanting.com for all the details, including a video of installing the columns.

Window Boxes and Wall Pots

Side-planted window boxes and wall pots are extremely useful.

The window boxes work well on fences or deck railings as well as under windows.

Wall pots work on any wall.

For easy hanging instructions, see the three minute video at www.sideplanting.com.

Stands and Columns that Support Baskets

The basic baskets can be hung or supported on stands or columns, which are easily planted in the garden. Patio stands can be used alone or planted in another container. See pages 130-133 to view it planted in a large container.

For easy installation instructions, see the three minute video at www.sideplanting.com.

Easy Planting: Side-Planted Container

Step 1

Spray the container with water to soften the coco fiber, if it feels too stiff.

Add potting mix up to the bottom of the first hole. ***Be sure to use top-quality potting mix with a brand name you trust. Do not use garden soil or top soil because these soils are too heavy and can kill the plants.***

Step 2

Remove the first side plant from the pot. Dip the roots in water, keeping them submerged until they are completely saturated. Remove the plant, and squeeze the root ball 3 to 6 times - *very* firmly - until most of the water has dripped out. (Plants with 4.5" root balls require more squeezing than plants with 3" root balls.) The root ball should be firm, not falling apart. If it still feels loose, squeeze it until it is quite firm.

(If some small pieces break off, that is ok - the plants we recommend are tough plants! I have had some root balls fall completely apart. I thought they would die but planted them anyway, and they did just fine!)

Step 3

Push the root ball through the first hole, from the outside in. Don't worry if some potting mix falls off the root ball. That is normal. Be sure the plant is on the outside of the container and the roots are on the inside. Adjust the flap so it fits between the roots and the plant.

You will see some open space between the plant and the top of the hole. That is normal. Very little potting mix escapes from this opening because the roots grow quickly, forming a solid mass.

Step 4

Alternate the three small plants around the sides. Fertilize with a slow-release mix, like the fertilizer described on page 46.

If your potting mix includes fertilizer, you can skip this step now, adding more only if the plants' leaves lose their color. However, I have found that the fertilizers included in the potting mixes don't last for long, so I add the better fertilizer when I plant.

The good, slow-release fertilizers usually last for the life of the basket.

Step 5

Remove the growing pot from the centerpiece and put the plant in the middle of the new container. Measure with your fingers to see how much potting mix you need to bring the top of the centerpiece's root ball to about 1/2" above the top edge of the container. Add the necessary potting mix, and place the centerpiece on top of it.

Add more potting mix around the centerpiece to bring the level up to about 1" below the rim of the pot.

Step 6

After soaking the first edge plant in water, squeeze it slightly between your hands to flatten it a bit - like a sandwich. Place it over a different plant - at an angle so that it leans slightly over the edge. Continue alternating plants until the edge is planted.

Add potting mix between the root balls, as well as on any exposed roots and pat it down slightly. Don't pile the potting mix up around the stems! Fertilize again. Do not water your finished container for about 3 days. Only water when the potting mix feels dry, or the plants are wilted.

For column installation instructions, go to www.sideplanting.com to see a 3-minute video called *Patio Stands and Border Columns*.

Easy Planting: Traditional Container

Step 1

Put some potting mix in the bottom of a pot with holes in it to ensure drainage. Without drainage, most plants die. If the holes are really large, cover with a layer of rock, coffee filter, or plastic screen to keep potting mix from escaping.

To see how much potting mix you'll need, hold the largest plant in the center so the top of the mix is about an inch below the top of the new pot. Remove the plant, and adjust the soil to reach that level.

Be sure to use top-quality potting mix with a brand name you trust. Do not use garden soil or top soil because these soils are too heavy and can kill the plants.

Step 2

To take the plant out of its pot, hold it upside down, and pull the pot off the root ball. If it resists, squeeze the sides of the pot and try again, or cut the pot off with garden shears.

If the roots are tightly wound in a circle, the plant is root-bound. It will grow better if you separate the roots. Untangle the roots slightly by breaking the tight circle apart. Repeat this action all around the root ball.

Step 3

Place the centerpiece plants in the middle of the container. These three dianthus make a full grouping. They are placed very close together, with root balls touching.

Check the level of the potting mix, and adjust it accordingly. Remember, you want the top of the root balls about an inch below the top of the new pot.

Step 4

Place the edge plants (in this case, coleus and torenia) around the centerpiece. Lean them out slightly, so you won't see soil from the top edge when the pot is done. Add more potting mix under these plants, if necessary, to keep all the root balls even on top.

Be sure to tilt the plants out a little, and keep the tops of their root balls even with the centerpiece. If they are not perfectly filled in, they will grow quickly!

Step 5

Once all the plants are placed, fill in any open spots between the root balls with potting mix. ***Don't pile the potting mix up around the stems or the plants could die It is all right for the root ball to be planted high, meaning slightly above the potting mix (see diagram on page 7).***

Sprinkle the fertilizer I describe on page 46 top of the potting mix. Apply the amount specified on the fertilizer box. If the mix already has fertilizer in it, you can skip the extra fertilizer now if you like. However, I have not found a potting mix with fertilizer that lasts the life of the plants, so I add some of my fertilizer anyway.

Step 6

Move the container to its final resting place before watering because it is lighter without the extra water. Water the container thoroughly and evenly (in a gentle stream with a watering can or hose nozzle) until you see water coming out of the drainage holes. After the pot has drained, add potting mix wherever it has settled. Enjoy!

Fertilizer

New Fertilizer is a No Brainer: Just Apply Once

Fertilizer is one of the most important components of blue ribbon plants and easy container gardens. Remember, the blue ribbon plants only require water after you plant them. But, that is possible <u>only</u> if you use a fertilizer at planting time that lasts the entire lifespan of the arrangement. Without fertilizer, the plants will slowly turn yellow and decline.

I have only found one fertilizer that works perfectly every time. And it is forgiving. If you use too much, it doesn't burn the plants. It also is excellent for the environment, winning the 2005 Gulf Guardian Award from the EPA Gulf of Mexico Program Partnership.

This fertilizer is slow-release, meaning its little pellets release the nutrients over a period of time. It is a great improvement over the liquids you apply weekly with a hose sprayer! However, there are many slow-release products on the market. I have tested every one I could get my hands on, and none come close to this one. Some either don't last as long or don't have all the nutrients plants need. Others release all their nutrients at once if there is a lot of rain, burning the plants.

This fertilizer lasts nine months in 'average' conditions. If you see the plants yellowing a bit, just add some more. Sprinkle it on top of the potting mix, following the instructions on the label.

Many potting mixes also include fertilizer. I haven't found one yet that lasts long, so I add this one at planting time as well. This fertilizer is available at www.kinsmangarden.com.

Look for These Ingredients on the Label

As I told you on page 8, I have killed many plants with the wrong fertilizer. I have also been through fertilizers that simply didn't make the grade. They included some but not all of the elements a plant needs. Weird, hard-to-diagnose nutritional deficiencies developed that were time consuming, annoying, and definitely not easy.

Plants are like people - they need lots of different nutrients to keep them alive. If you have a vitamin deficiency, you might get quite sick. Same thing for a plant. Learn to read the fertilizer label to make sure it includes *all* the nutrients your plants need.

Most fertilizers include nitrogen, phosphorus (phosphate), and potassium (potash). Most, including some of the best-selling brands, don't include the micronutrients that plants need. ***So look for boron, copper, iron, manganese, and magnesium as well. Do not buy a product that doesn't include these micronutrients, or your plants could suffer later.***

All of the containers in this book were fertilized once at planting time with my fertilizer. The container (left) features a ti plant in the center with caladiums and dwarf chenille plants around the edges. The pool container features a jatropha in the center, surrounded by crotons, coleus, and creeping Jenny.

Watering Basics

General

Watering takes the most time of any container garden chore. Plants in containers need more water than plants in the ground because their root systems are smaller, and the roots are where plants store most of their water. The root system of a plant in the ground is three times the diameter of the plant. Not so for container plants - the roots are only as large as the container.

I was pleasantly surprised by the watering needs of side-planted containers. Prior to using them, I was concerned that the coco fiber liner would not hold water for long. I pictured myself permanently standing next to a container pouring water on it! Luckily, that was not the case. Read these two pages to learn what it took me hundreds of trials to master.

Water with a Gentle Stream

Check out the nozzle on the watering wand shown above. This nozzle diffuses the water, so you don't blow the little plants right out of the pots. The same effect comes from a nozzle that fits directly on the hose. I like the hose nozzles that have a lot of different settings, so I can use a gentle stream for soaking a container or a strong stream for cleaning a patio.

Factors That Affect Water Use

❀ **Sun or shade.** Plants use one-third to one-half as much water in shade than in full sun.

❀ **Temperature.** Plants use more water when the temperatures are high.

❀ **Wind.** Plants in windy areas require more water than plants in calm areas.

❀ **Reflections from walls.** If you have a light-colored wall facing south with no shade, you may have to plant succulents to take the reflected heat if you live in a very hot climate.

❀ **Soil.** Good-quality potting mix usually includes peat moss, which holds water better than cheaper, sandy soils.

❀ **Plant type.** Plant species vary in their need for water. Impatiens, for example, need much more water than cactus.

❀ **Container size.** Large containers with small plants require much less water than small containers filled to the brim with large plants.

❀ **How long the plant has been in the container.** As plants age in containers, their roots fill the pot, leaving less space for water.

How to Tell When a Plant Needs Water

Water when you see signs of wilt, or the soil feels dry to the touch. Use your finger to test the soil. Push it into the soil about an inch or so. Low-water plants, like cacti and succulents, need less water and can go longer with dry soil.

Knowing when to water is very important because many container plants die from overwatering. If the plant looks wilted and the soil has been wet for several days, the plant is drowning and will probably die. It has a fungus. You might try a fungicide if the plant is very important to you.

How Much Water to Apply

Water thoroughly with each application. The biggest watering mistake people make is to give the plant just a little bit of water. That is the same as giving a person dying of thirst just a teaspoonful of water! Soak the plant thoroughly until you see a steady stream of water coming out of the bottom of the pot. A slow soaking is better than a fast hit with the hose because it allows the roots time to absorb the water.

Re-Hydrating Really Dry Plants

Plants in a severe state of wilt that look like they are near death may benefit from a bottom-soaking. The soil is dry and has shrunk away from the sides of the pot, and when you water from the top, the water just washes down between the sides of the pot and the soil. In addition, the soil feels hard, like a chunk of wood, and is not absorbing the water. If this is the case, put the whole pot on top of a container of water - a saucer or baking pan is ideal. Leave it overnight. The water will be absorbed by the soil like a sponge, and your plant will probably be quite healthy in the morning!

Water Needs Change as a Plant Ages

Plants need a lot of water right after they are planted. Then, as the roots grow, the plant needs less water. Once the roots fill the pot, the plant needs more water again!

Watering Shortcuts

Shade Containers Require MUCH Less Water than Sun Containers!

I have been amazed at how little water shade containers need compared to their sun counterparts. This window box needed water about once a week. It is large (36" side-planted, from www.kinsman-garden.com) and I used potting mix that included moisture-retaining granules.

The sun baskets that were near this window box needed water every day! That means this shade container required SEVEN TIMES less water than those in direct sun!

Think how hot you feel on a sunny day in August when you are standing in full sun. Step into the shade, and you will feel much cooler. Plants feel the same thing and need much less water in the cooler conditions that shade provides.

Plant One Inch Below the Rim to Make Watering Easier

Watering is easier if you have some room between the top of the soil and the edge of the pot. Water can pool in this space and drip into the soil slowly, so you don't have to stand there giving the plant a little bit of water at a time until you see it drain out of the bottom. This is easy to do in large pots but harder in small ones that are packed full of plants.

Low-Water Plants

Different kinds of plants need different amounts of water. The group that required the least amount of water in my trials were succulents and cacti. They store more water in their roots and leaves than most other plants.

I've had great luck with these incredibly easy plants when grown in containers. They are becoming the rage of the gardening world. This new-found popularity is causing garden centers to increase their stocks of these wonderful plants. This container was NEVER watered during its entire 18 month lifespan (it received rainwater at least once every two weeks)!

Automatic Drip Systems

This is the best idea I have for easy container gardens. Install an automatic system with a timer and never drag a hose around again! I will never go through another summer without one!

Drip irrigation hooks up to your hose or sprinkler system and has an emitter for each pot. Systems are easily available in kit form and fairly easy to install, or your sprinkler repairman can install them for you. These systems greatly reduce the time spent watering but do require some maintenance because the emitters can fall out of the pots or become clogged. There are many different types of emitters available, so be sure yours fit the size of your pots. Some emitters are designed for very small pots, for example, and won't deliver enough water to a large container. Drip systems are designed to water a lot of pots at once, which can be a disadvantage if only one plant needs it, and the others don't.

Water-holding Polymers

Many companies are developing water-holding gels (like Terrasorb or Hortasorb) to hold water in containers longer. These materials look like rock salt when they are dry. They absorb water and expand into a jello-like substance when soaked in water. A tablespoon of polymer expands to about a quart of wet material. It is added to the potting soil before planting. Desire Foard, owner of Gardenstyle and creator of the beautiful container gardens along the streets in Naples, uses these materials in most of her containers. They cut her watering chores down by about one third. She saturates the material in water for 10 to 15 minutes before adding it to the potting soil. It is very important to wet it before you add it to the soil. One lady told me all her plants died after she tried the polymers. My guess is that she either added it dry or added too much. Be sure to follow the instructions to the letter on the box.

Many potting mixes now include water-holding polymers. All the potting mixes I use include them (except the mixes I use for succulents), and I have had excellent luck with them. The brands I have tried cut watering down by about one-third.

I have heard reports of potting mixes with water-holding polymers retaining too much water, causing the plants to rot. Although I have not yet had any negative results with these mixes, I've only tried them in very dry years. The jury is still out as to how they perform in rainy years.

Large Pots

Large pots hold more potting mix than smaller ones, so they require less water. This pot is a full 30 inches tall. I have had it for years planted with the canna lilies you see here. I have gone for weeks on end without watering it at all! I leave the cannas in all year. They die back in the winter and reappear the following spring in Georgia (zone 7). I never water them at all in the winter.

When I add edge plants that require more water, like these lime green sweet potato plants, I water more, about twice a week. Smaller pots filled with sweet potato plants in the same place would require water every day!

Grooming and Displaying

Pinching and Trimming

Before Pinching | Pinching to Smooth Bulge | After Pinching

If plants look leggy or uneven, pinch or trim off the unwanted portions. Use your finger or pruning shears (if the stem is too thick).

See the plant profiles for individual pinching and cut-back requirements.

The plant in the first photo has a bulge on the right side near the top. It is easy to pinch the plants to even it out. The plant looks best if you trim just about the juncture of two leaves.

See www.sideplanting.com for a short video called *Fertilization and Trimming*. It only lasts about two minutes and shows you this technique.

Replacing Plants

Before | During | After

Sometimes one plant dies in a mixed container while the others are still thriving. Simply remove the dead plant and replace it with a new one. Even though this unsightly plant is not quite dead, it needs replacing.

First, wet the soil and try to gently remove the roots with your hand. If the roots resist, get a small trowel and gently cut around the roots of the plant. Try not to disturb the roots of the other plants any more than is necessary.

Second, plant the new plant in its place. Fertilize with your slow-release fertilizer.

Look at the difference in the before and after photos! One unsightly plant had completely ruined the look of this container.

Displaying Containers

Pot feet

Pot feet

I seldom use saucers under my pots. They hold water and sometimes keep the plant too wet. I will occasionally bring them out to use in very hot weather, however, because I'm not worried about too wet but rather too dry in our summer heat.

It's a good idea to use little 'pot feet' (shown above from www.kinsmangarden.com) or some sort of stand to keep the pot off the ground. I don't worry about this with pots in the garden but like them when pots are on hardscapes, such as wood, brick, or concrete. Sometimes I can't find one that looks good with the pot and in that case, I don't worry about it. I am noticing wood rot on my wood deck where I have had large containers directly on the wood for a few years.

Low plant stands on wheels are very useful. They keep the pot off the ground and make it easy to move. If pots are against a building or wall, they need to be turned so that all sides get some light. Wheels make this quite easy, especially with heavy pots.

Turn your Hanging Baskets

Hanging baskets should be rotated for even growth if one side has more light than another. Swivel hooks allow you to do this without taking them off the hook. The Swivlit (shown left, from www.kinsmangarden.com) works for 14 and 16 inch baskets (up to 55 pounds). Use a larger one (right) for larger baskets. I found this one at my home improvement store.

Odds and Ends

Separating Bromeliads

Bromeliads are one of the easiest plants I know. They are rapidly gaining popularity and are commonly available in the house plant section of your garden center. In frost free areas, bromeliads are also popular landscape plants. They flower for a few months a year. After a bromeliad flowers, it produces offshoots (baby bromeliads) at the base. The mother plant dies when the babies are grown. When the babies are half as big as the mother plant, they can be separated. It is easy! Many gardeners overwinter these babies inside the house. Some will re-flower the next warm season, but some will not.

1. Remove the bromeliad clump from its container.

2. Cut them apart. This is really fool-proof. I have never lost one!

3. Even if they have no roots, most will survive.

4. The three plants are ready for planting.

5. Here are the plants in their containers. When they are this small, I store them in an out-of-the-way place until they grow large enough to make attractive, full plants.

Pest Control

I seldom use pesticides on container plants. Many pesticides are quite toxic and are capable of killing you as well as the pest. Before using any pesticide, type the name of it into an internet search engine and push 'go.' Read about it to understand its risks. Occasionally, I use fungicide after rainy periods, and I routinely use snail bait with sweet potato vines. If I see holes in the leaves, I leave the plant alone unless it becomes severe. Holes are often caused by snails or caterpillars, which feed at night when you can't see them. Take the leaf to your garden center, and ask them for the least-toxic alternative. Be sure the plant is not a larval food plant for butterflies.

Japanese beetles are the plague of my Georgia garden. They arrive in a swarm in the spring, and rapidly devour many plants, including sweet potato vines and New Guinea impatiens. They nest in the lawn. Have the lawn sprayed by a pro in the fall, so they don't hatch the next spring. If they do come, don't use bait because it only attracts more. Ask your garden center for the least toxic spray.

Splitting Rootballs

Vining plants with roots that clump can often be split or pulled apart so you can use one plant in several different locations. I frequently split pots of creeping Jenny, ivy, and silver licorice. Ivy can also be pulled apart by the roots into even smaller pieces.

1. After removing the plant from its container, soak the roots in water until it is really soaked.

2. Gently pull the roots apart. (Once, before I knew better, I cut a root ball in two with a steak knife, but it worked just fine!)

3. Now you have two plants instead of just one!

Soaking Rootballs to Reduce Their Size

Throughout this book, you see containers that are very full. One of the professional tricks to filling a container to the brim on planting day is to soak the roots of the plants in water prior to planting them. This soaking allows you to squeeze them into smaller shapes.

This can be hard to get used to for the novice. I talk a lot about proper spacing in my landscaping books with plants planted in the ground. Generally, you leave quite a bit of space between the plants to give them room to grow when planting them in the ground. This is very important for long-term landscapes.

But most container gardens are designed for short-term, maximum impact. Most people don't want to wait six months for the container on their front steps to look good. Soaking the roots can assist in yielding instant, full results.

Vegetables in Containers

It is easier to grow vegetables in containers than in the ground. I plan to test many in the future, but for now my trials have been limited to decorative plants.

The best book I know for growing vegetables in containers is *McGee & Stuckey's Bountiful Container* by Rose Marie Nichols McGee and Maggie Stuckey.

Chapter 2

One Plant Wonders

Fabulous container gardens do not have to be complicated. Sometimes, simplicity is the best choice. Nothing is simpler than one plant in a pot.

Ideas for one plant wonders:
- ❀ Plant one type of plant in a fabulous container.
- ❀ Plant a fabulous plant, like an orchid, in any simple container.
- ❀ Repeat the same kind of container with the same plant, as shown.

Above: Three glazed bowls filled with double impatiens. These high performers are excellent plants for shade color because they are easy to grow, dependable, and have a long bloom period.

These low bowls are great for quick impact, but impatiens flowers will need larger containers within about three months of planting. You can cut them back (to about four inches tall) when they get too big, which could be easier than replanting. However, you'll have to wait about a month for them to rebloom.

Left: This is one of the best, blue ribbon ideas in this book! Just plant dragon wing begonias in big blue pots! I have had red ones in these three pots on either side of my entry walk for three summers in a row. They get huge - reaching a full four feet tall by the end of the season.

Unique New Color

This arrangement rates a red ribbon (defined on pages 18-19) because it requires one additional chore other than watering: monthly trimming, which only takes about five minutes! However, this coleus lasts at least the five-to-six month red ribbon minimum in this large container, and the arrangement was trouble free. Be sure to follow the easy planting instructions on pages 44-45.

I bought this plant specifically for this gorgeous pot, colored with a green called "Swamp." New pot colors arrive at garden centers each spring, and it is fun to collect a variety of colors. That way, you always have the right pot handy for whatever plant catches your fancy.

Many of the coleus I grew behaved differently in different sized pots. Their leaves grew substantially larger in larger containers. However, even the largest coleus adapted well to smaller containers but didn't last as long.

'Crime Scene' Coleus
(1 plant from a three-gallon pot)
Plant Profile: Page 148

Cultural Information

Light: Light shade to full sun

Season: Spring through fall for most warmer areas. This plant takes temperatures from about 40 degrees to the low 100's and is equally happy in either extreme.

Lifespan: Five to six months in this container

Care: Fertilize on planting day with a slow-release mix described on page 46. Repeat if the leaves look yellowish or washed-out, although the fertilizer should last from six to nine months.

Trim the coleus to keep it looking tight.

For my three minute trimming video, see *Fertilization and Trimming* at www.sideplanting.com.

Water: Water thoroughly if the plants show signs of wilt, or the soil feels dry when you push your fingertip into the potting mix (see pages 48-49). I watered this one every day (after it was about a month old) in mid summer and every other day in cooler weather. See pages 50-51 to learn about watering shortcuts.

Troubleshooting: No problems at all

Planting Plan: Easy. Simply plant a large coleus in the center of the pot. Be sure to plant in good-quality potting <u>mix</u>, not garden soil, top soil, or potting soil, which can kill your plants. Other important planting tips are shown on pages 44-45.

Container: Anamese's *Milan Short Square*, medium (18.5"H x 13"W), swamp. Shop for it at www.anamese.com.

The copper colored pots at the same web site are excellent companions for this unique, swamp green.

If you can't find this exact container, check out local garden centers to see the latest glazes. They are getting more diverse each year!

Eclectic Combination

This container didn't rate a ribbon strictly because I don't have enough experience with diascia - only one season. However, it really did well, blooming for a full five months during cooler temperatures that averaged 50 to 60 degrees at night and 75 to 85 degrees in the daytime.

I never would have thought this plant could look good in this container unless I had tried it. The pot is formal and seems appropriate for formal plantings, like topiaries. However, it looks great filled with informal diascia. I really like having a collection of different pots at home, so I can try plants in them for new and exciting looks.

Diascia 'Miracle'
(1 plant from a one-gallon pot)
Plant Profile: Page 167

Cultural Information

Light: Light shade to full sun

Season: Plant when the temperatures range from 40 to 85 degrees. I haven't tried it in cooler or hotter weather.

Lifespan: Four to six months in this container

Care: Fertilize on planting day with a slow-release mix (see page 46 for correct type). Repeat if the leaves look yellowish or washed-out, although the fertilizer should last from six to nine months. That's it! This is a really easy design.

Water: Water thoroughly if the plants show signs of wilt, or the soil feels dry when you push your fingertip into the potting mix (see pages 48-49). I watered this one every two to three days. See pages 50-51 to learn about watering shortcuts.

Troubleshooting: No problems at all

Planting Plan: Easy. Simply plant the diascia in the center of the pot. Be sure to plant in good-quality potting mix, not garden soil, top soil, or potting soil, which can kill your plants. Other important planting tips are shown on pages 44-45.

Container: Campania's cast stone *Rappallo Garland Urn* in CH finish, 17"W x 22.5"H.

Although cast stone is quite heavy, it is an excellent choice for windy locations because it takes hurricane force winds to blow it over!

Shop for it at www.campaniainternational.com or check out local sources. Since these pots are heavy, you pay quite a price for freight to bring them into your area from elsewhere. Look in your yellow pages under "Stone - cast," and call the companies to see if they make pots. Many cast stone companies specialize in columns or fountains and might not make pots. Look for crisp detailing (not blurry!) and barely visible seams.

Unique and Easy

1ST

This combination is a great example of an easy container garden - it's easy to design, plant, and maintain! It rates a blue ribbon (defined on pages 14-17) because, after planting it properly, it requires nothing but water and lasts for at least five to six months. To get this high performance, be sure to follow the easy planting instructions on pages 44-45. As an added bonus, if you live in zones 5-11, plant the grass in your garden when it has outgrown the pot.

This handcrafted iron container combines unique container material with a terrific, contemporary design that resembles sculpture. It comes in either a natural rust or powder coat finish. We tested the natural rust and are thrilled with its appearance after eighteen months outside. During its five-to-ten year lifespan, it has continued to oxidize, becoming quite rustic in appearance.

Fountain grass is one of the easiest plants around. The fuzzy things on top are actually flowers and are not there all the time. However, even without the fuzzy blooms, the grass is quite attractive.

Fountain Grass
(2 plants from three-gallon pot)
Plant Profile: Page 153

Cultural Information

Light: Light shade to full sun

Season: Spring through fall for most areas. This plant takes temperatures from about 40 degrees to the low 100's and is equally happy in either extreme.

Lifespan: At least six months in this container. Transplant it to your garden after it outgrows the pot if you live in zones 5-11.

Care: Fertilize on planting day with the slow-release mix described on page 46. That's it! This is a really easy design.

Water: Water thoroughly if the soil feels dry when you push your fingertip into the potting mix (see pages 48-49). I watered this twice a week in mid summer and once a week in cooler weather. See pages 50-51 to learn about watering shortcuts.

Troubleshooting: No problems at all

Planting Plan: Easy. Plant two fountain grasses side by side. I used large ones from three gallon pots so the pot would look filled in from day one. Be sure to plant in good quality potting <u>mix</u>, not garden soil, top soil, or potting soil, which can kill your plants. Other important planting tips are shown on pages 44-45.

Container: Ore's #117 Vertical Window Box (33"L x 14"D x 40"H). Shop for it at www.orecontainers.com.

1ST

This arrangement rates a blue ribbon (defined on pages 14-17) because, after planting it properly, it requires nothing but water for at least six months. And, it lasts for many more years in this large container if you follow the easy planting and fertilizing instructions on pages 44-45.

Dieffenbachia is an old-fashioned house plant that is almost indestructible. Although it is shown here in a tropical garden, it flourishes anywhere the temperatures stay above 45 degrees, provided it grows in shade. It is not a showy plant, so display it in fabulous containers, like these bright-colored columns.

One of my readers' most frequent questions is what to plant in deep shade - places so dark that even weeds won't grow. Choices are limited because most plants prefer more light, but dieffenbachia is a definitely a great choice. Check out the house plant section of your garden center for more good choices. Since most of them are green, use colored containers if you prefer more color in your shady garden.

Dieffenbachia
(1 plant from a three-gallon pot)
Plant Profile: Page 150

Cultural Information

Light: Dense, medium, or light shade

Season: Spring, summer, or fall. Dieffenbachia won't tolerate temperatures under 40 degrees. Does quite well indoors.

Lifespan: Dieffenbachia lasts for many years in a pot this large if it is protected from temperatures under 40 degrees.

Care: Fertilize on planting day with the slow-release mix described on page 46. Repeat every six to nine months.

Water: Water thoroughly if the soil feels dry when you push your fingertip into the potting mix (see pages 48-49). I watered this once a week in mid summer and every ten days in cooler weather. Since the pot is in shade, it requires much less water than containers growing in sun.

Troubleshooting: Dieffenbachia is poisonous to humans and animals because it contains oxalate. Eating the plant, even in small quantities, results in burning and swelling of the mouth and throat. In larger doses, effects are quite serious, possibly life threatening. However, if no one eats the leaves, the plant causes no harm.

Planting Plan: Easy. Plant a nice sized dieffenbachia in the middle of the pot so that it looks filled in immediately. Be sure to plant in good-quality potting <u>mix</u>, not garden soil, top soil, or potting soil, which can kill your plants.

Container: Anamese's *Tall Milan* pots in aqua, blue, and green (36.5"H x 15.5" W). Shop for them at www.anamese.com.

Tall, columnar pots raise plants to eye level. This height makes it easier to appreciate both the plants and the fabulous glazes on the pots.

Additional Comments: I don't replace all the potting mix in a container this size each time I replant in it - only about the top 15 inches. Don't try styrofoam pellets in the bottom - they are biodegradable and disintegrate after the first watering!

Chapter 3

Two Plant Combos

Designing with just two plants is quite easy. This chapter will give you lots of ideas! Great looking container gardens don't have to be complicated! The majority of two plant combinations feature a centerpiece in the middle surrounded by smaller plants. This is a great way for beginners to learn container gardening.

Above: The green containers are planted with hot pink pentas and purple heliotrope. They are in a flower bed surrounded by white torenia to define them. Yellow melampodium and blue torenia are planted in the foreground.

Left: The cobalt blue tall column has phormium (flax) as a centerpiece, surrounded by white double wave petunias. The smaller blue container features coleus as a centerpiece, surrounded by the same petunias.

This was my first and, so far, only try with the new double wave petunias. I was quite happy with their performance. I had thought that the dead flowers would look brown and ugly, and require hand removal. However, this was not the case. They seemed to disappear on their own with no work at all! So, all I had to do was add water to these beautiful plants. They didn't last as long as I would have liked - only three months. But I will definitely use them again. The flowers are just gorgeous! And these blue containers are plenty large enough to support the plants for the entire growing season.

Simple Arrangement

What a great idea for cobalt blue pots! This simple arrangement of red double impatiens surrounded by yellow calibrachoa (or million bells) is all this pot needs to become a striking combination. Although the double impatiens are fabulous container plants, the calibrachoa is an erratic performer, so the arrangement didn't rate a ribbon. Some calibrachoa varieties I tried did quite well, while others only lasted a month or two.

If you find a good calibrachoa cultivar, this arrangement is very easy to care for. The impatiens filled in quickly, but the calibrachoa were planted small and took a few months to trail over the edge of the pot.

Cobalt blue pots are naturals for red and yellow flowers of all types.

Yellow Calibrachoa or Million Bells
(8 plants from 4" pots)
Plant Profile: Page 168

Double Impatiens
(3 plants from one-gallon pots)
Plant Profile: Page 155

Cultural Information

Light: Light shade is ideal for most areas. Takes full sun in cool, short, frost-free days, like the winter in south Florida.

Season: Plant when temperatures vary between 40 and 90 degrees. The calibrachoa do not do well in higher heat.

Lifespan: Five to six months in this container if the calibrachoa is a good cultivar.

Care: Fertilize on planting day with the slow-release mix I describe on page 46. Repeat if the leaves look yellowish or washed out.

Both flowers drop a lot. The impatiens are particularly hard to remove from pavement.

Water: Water thoroughly when plants show signs of wilt, or the soil feels dry when you push your fingertip into the potting mix (see pages 48-49). I watered this one every three days in spring and every day in the heat of summer. Impatiens require quite a bit of water. See pages 50-51 to learn about watering shortcuts.

Troubleshooting: These flowers drop a lot, which require a lot of clean-up if you use them on pavement.

Planting Plan: Easy. Plant the impatiens in the middle, and surround them with calibrachoa. Be sure to plant in good-quality potting <u>mix</u>, not garden soil, top soil, or potting soil, which can kill your plants. Other important planting tips are shown on pages 44-45.

Container: I bought this pot from a roadside vendor four years ago. It is still going strong!

Cannas and Dragon Wings

2ND

One qualification for a blue ribbon is a degree of resistance to pests. Since the canna lilies frequently attract pests, this arrangement rates a red ribbon instead. In this container, the cannas needed to be sprayed once for beetles. I also groomed them occasionally, removing dead leaves. Other than that, I only added water for its six month lifespan! To get this high performance, be sure to follow the easy planting instructions on pages 44-45.

I experimented last year and left the cannas outside in the pots all winter. The leaves died in the first freeze. However, I was quite excited the following spring to see leaves sprouting! The temperatures got down to about 15 degrees during the winter.

This tall container looks good with a centerpiece that follows the same form. The canna lily is the perfect shape for this container.

Canna Lily
(1 plant from a one-gallon pot)
Plant Profile: Page 147

Dragon Wing Begonia
(8 plants from 4.5" pots)
Plant Profile: Page 145

Cultural Information

Light: Full sun is ideal.

Season: Grow this arrangement in warm to hot temperatures, from about 65 to over 100 degrees. The dragon wing begonia will take cooler temperatures, down to 33 degrees.

Lifespan: Five to six months in this container.

Care: Fertilize on planting day with the slow-release mix I describe on page 46. Repeat if the leaves look yellowish or washed-out. Groom the cannas by trimming off dead leaves. If you have time, trim off the old flowers as well.

Water: Water thoroughly when plants show signs of wilt, or the soil feels dry when you push your fingertip into the potting mix (see pages 48-49). Containers as large as this one don't require water as often as smaller ones. I watered this one twice a week in spring and fall and every other day in the heat of summer. See pages 50-51 to learn about watering shortcuts.

Troubleshooting: Japanese beetles attacked the cannas once. I sprayed the plants with pesticide.

Planting Plan: Easy. Plant the canna lily in the center and surround it with the begonias. Other important planting tips are shown on pages 44-45.

Container: Anamese's *Tall Milan* pot in green (36.5"H x 15.5" W). Shop for it at www.anamese.com.

Tall, columnar pots raise plants to eye level. This height makes it easier to appreciate both the plants and the fabulous glazes on the pots.

Additional Comments: I don't replace all the potting mix in a container this size each time I replant in it - only about the top 15 inches. Don't try styrofoam pellets in the bottom - they are biodegradable and disintegrate after the first watering!

Great for Land or Sea!

This bromeliad arrangement rates a blue ribbon (defined on pages 14-17) because it requires nothing but water after planting it properly. And, even though the container is too small to support most container gardens for six to nine months, bromeliads have small root systems and thrive for that long in this low bowl. To get this high performance, be sure to follow the easy planting instructions on pages 44-45.

I took this container with me to the garden center and had them help me with the composition. We used gravel on top of the potting mix to add a nice, finishing touch.

This container would do well in many different environments. While many bromeliads don't like direct sun and salt spray, some do, like these that have very thick leaves.

Bromeliad
(1 plant from a one-gallon pot)
Plant Profile: Page 146

Bromeliad
(6 plants from 4" pots)
Plant Profile: Page 146

Cultural Information

Light: Full sun to medium shade, which is unusual for bromeliads. Most prefer shade.

Season: Grow this arrangement in warm to hot temperatures, from about 33 to over 100 degrees.

Lifespan: Six to nine months in this container. You can tell they need transplanting because they will look like they are falling out of the pot.

Single plants live for about two years but send up babies to replace themselves, provided they are protected from frost. See page 54 to learn how to separate the babies.

The flower lasts about three to four months.

Care: Fertilize on planting day with the slow-release mix I describe on page 46. Repeat every six months. Put the fertilizer in the potting mix around the plants, not in the center cup. Trim off dead leaves and flowers occasionally. These are really easy plants!

Water: These are low water plants. Water them thoroughly when the potting mix feels really dry, about every week or so (see pages 48-49). Water the potting mix instead of the center well of the plant.

Troubleshooting: Some bromeliads, these included, have sharp spines.

Planting Plan: Easy. Plant the large bromeliad in the center and surround it with the smaller ones. Be sure to plant in good-quality potting <u>mix</u>, not garden soil, top soil, or potting soil, which can kill your plants. Other important planting tips are shown on pages 44-45.

Container: Low, aqua bowl made of glazed clay

Traditional Flowers

This arrangement misses a ribbon for two reasons. First, the plants bloom most but not all of the time. Second, they require deadheading (trimming off dead flowers) in order to look their best. However, that doesn't stop me from using these plants frequently. Blue plumbago, a tropical perennial that is used as an annual in most areas, forms the centerpiece. It is a great choice for heat, along with the pink pentas that are planted in the front.

The yellow container is a perfect contrast to the blue and pink flowers.

Pentas are one of the best flowers for attracting butterflies.

Butterfly Pentas
(3 plants from 4.5" pots)
Plant Profile: Page 159

Plumbago
(1 plant from a three-gallon pot)
Plant Profile: Page 169

Cultural Information

Light: Full sun to light shade is ideal.

Season: Grow when the temperatures range from 75 to over 100 degrees. Although the plumbago lives in temperatures that are much lower, it doesn't bloom unless it is quite warm.

Lifespan: About four months in this container. These plants would live longer in a larger container.

Care: Fertilize on planting day with the slow-release mix I describe on page 46. Repeat every six to nine months or if the leaves look yellowish or washed-out. The pentas bloom more if the old blooms are removed.

If you live in zones 9-11, you can plant the plumbago in the ground after it outgrows the container. It is a very satisfactory landscape plant in warm areas.

Water: Water thoroughly when plants show signs of wilt, or the soil feels dry when you push your fingertip into the potting mix (see pages 48-49). I watered this one about every other day in light shade and up to every day in full sun. See pages 50-51 to learn about watering shortcuts.

Troubleshooting: No problems

Planting Plan: Easy. Plant the plumbago in the center, along the back edge of the pot. Fill in the front with the pentas. Be sure to plant in good quality potting mix, not garden soil, top soil, or potting soil, which can kill your plants. Other important planting tips are shown on pages 44-45.

I soaked the rootballs in water to reduce their size prior to planting so that the container would look full immediately. See page 54 for more on this technique.

Container: Global Pottery's *Fleur De Lis* in French Yellow (16"H x 13"W). Shop for it at www.globalpottery.com.

Don't Be Shy with Color!

1ST

Combining bright blue, yellow, and red is about as bright as you can get in this blue ribbon arrangement (defined on pages 14-17). It blooms continuously for at least five months and requires no care at all other than water. To get this high performance, be sure to follow the easy planting instructions on pages 44-45, and use a pot large enough to sustain these plants for a full season (at least 20 inches wide).

The container is so bright it almost vibrates with color. Although the chenille plant (small tree with fuzzy flowers) might be difficult to find in your area, the concept is easy to copy with many other plants. Garden centers are usually stocked full of small trees that fit well in containers.

Chenille Plant
(1 plant from a 15-gallon pot)
Plant Profile: Page 148

Melampodium
(10 plants from 4.5" pots)
Plant Profile: Page 157

Cultural Information

Light: Light shade to full sun

Season: These plants like it hot! Plant them in temperatures from 80 to over 100 degrees. Although they live in lower temperatures (down to 40 degrees without leaf burn), they flower more when it is hot.

Lifespan: The chenille tree will live for many years in a container this large if it is protected from frost. Melampodium is an annual, living about five or six months.

Care: Fertilize on planting day with the slow-release mix I describe on page 46. Repeat every six to nine months or if the leaves look yellowish or washed out. The chenille tree can be planted in the garden after it has outgrown the pot, if you live in zones 10-11.

Water: Water thoroughly when plants show signs of wilt, or the soil feels dry when you push your fingertip into the potting mix (see pages 48-49). The great thing about using a container this large is that you don't have to water it anywhere near as much as smaller ones. I watered this one about twice a week until the temperatures got really hot (over 90 degrees), when I increased it to every other day.

Troubleshooting: No problems. This was a wonderful, trouble-free arrangement.

Planting Plan: Easy. Plant the chenille in the center, and surround it with melampodium. The container looks full immediately if you use the sizes shown on the photos to the left. Other important planting tips are shown on pages 44-45.

Container: This container is HUGE - I don't think the photo shows how big it is. It is one of my largest, weighing in at 150 pounds! Once you get it in place, you certainly don't have to worry about it blowing away! I left it outside last winter, and it didn't crack at 15 degrees. It is Campania International's *Anduze Urn* (27"W X 31"H). Shop for it at www.campaniainternational.com

Color in Fiberglass Container

This arrangement features blue ribbon plants, but the pot is a bit too small (13" wide) to support the growth of these plants for full season, so it misses a ribbon. However, if the container was at least 16 to 18 inches wide, it would qualify for a blue ribbon.

A jatropha tree sits in the middle of the container, surrounded by crotons. These are tropical plants that are becoming more popular as container plants in cooler climates. You'll probably see the croton in your garden center but not the jatropha. Substitute one of the many patio trees that are common in most garden centers at the beginning of your growing season.

This container is actually fiberglass, but it is a dead ringer for metal. Fiberglass is lighter, easier to clean, and lasts longer than metal.

Jatropha
(1 plant from a seven-gallon pot)
Plant Profile: Page 168

Mammey Crotons
(6 plants from three-gallon pots)
Plant Profile: Page 149

Cultural Information

Light: Full sun is ideal.

Season: The jatropha tree blooms in temperatures from about 65 to over 100 degrees. Crotons have color all the time. Protect both plants from frost. They are quite happy in heat.

Lifespan: Three to five months in this container. They would last longer in a larger container.

Plant them in your landscape if you live in zone 10-11, after they outgrow the container.

Many gardeners over-winter their crotons inside their houses.

Care: Fertilize on planting day with the slow-release mix I describe on page 46. Repeat every six to nine months or if the leaves look yellowish or washed out.

Water: Water thoroughly when plants show signs of wilt, or the soil feels dry when you push your fingertip into the potting mix (see pages 48-49). I watered this one about twice a week in cooler temperatures (under 85 degrees) to every other day in full sun and hot temperatures. See pages 50-51 to learn about watering shortcuts.

Troubleshooting: No problems. This was a wonderful, trouble-free arrangement.

Planting Plan: Easy. Plant the jatropha in the center, and surround it with the crotons. Use the sizes shown left to insure instant fullness. Be sure to plant in good-quality potting <u>mix</u>, not garden soil, top soil, or potting soil, which can kill the plants. Other important planting tips are shown on pages 44-45.

I soaked the rootballs in water to reduce their size prior to planting. See page 54 for more on this technique.

Container: Global Pottery's *Fiberglass Lattice Box* (16"H x 13"W). Shop for it at www.globalpottery.com.

Chapter 4

Three Plant Combos

Many container gardeners love the design challenge of mixing at least thee plants in a container. It is a wonderful opportunity for self expression. Here are some tips that might help:

✿ Choose your combinations at the garden center. It is easiest to see which plants you like together by actually holding them next to one another.

✿ Use your design instinct. Whatever leads you to choose a particular shirt in combination with a pair of slacks or a throw pillow for your couch is your design instinct. Luckily, it's easy to find! Simply see which plant combinations make you smile!

✿ Be sure to choose plants that like the same growing conditions.

Left and above: Pink and purple pansies mixed with lime green creeping Jenny grace these containers. Notice the power of repetition! Nine containers planted with the same plants! What could be easier?

Photos from Gibbs Gardens in Ball Ground, Georgia

Consider Leaf Color

2ND

One qualification for a blue ribbon is no maintenance at all after planting other than watering. This arrangement misses a blue ribbon only because the coleus needs monthly trimming, which takes about five minutes a month! Other than that, these plants are just about as easy as it gets. They have no problem living through a long, six month season in this good-sized pot (16 inch diameter). To get this high performance, be sure to follow the easy planting instructions on pages 44-45.

The red and yellow leaves of the coleus really make this container pop, particularly since it is planted in a red container. The flowers of the golden shrimp plant add to the color.

Golden Shrimp Plant
(1 plant from a three-gallon pot)
Plant Profile: Page 162

'Defiance' Coleus
(5 plants from 4.5" pots)
Plant Profile: Page 148

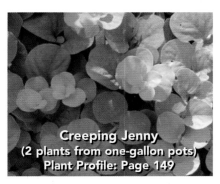

Creeping Jenny
(2 plants from one-gallon pots)
Plant Profile: Page 149

Cultural Information

Light: Light shade is ideal, particularly if the temperatures climb into the mid-80's or higher. This plant combination takes full sun in temperatures ranging from 45 to about 85 degrees.

Season: Plant when the temperatures range from 45 degrees to the low 100's. This arrangement tolerates both extremes well.

Lifespan: Five to six months in this container

Care: Fertilize on planting day with the slow-release mix I describe on page 46. Repeat if the leaves look yellowish or washed out. Pinch the coleus if it gets too tall and to keep the creeping Jenny from spreading all over the brick. I trimmed this one about once a month. For my three minute trimming video, see *Fertilization and Trimming* at www.sideplanting.com.

Once the plants outgrow this container, the shrimp plant will grow in your garden if you live in zones 9-11. The creeping Jenny thrives in the ground in zones 3-8.

Water: Water thoroughly when plants show signs of wilt, or the soil feels dry when you push your fingertip into the potting mix (see pages 48-49). I watered this every three days in spring and every day in the heat of summer.

Troubleshooting: No problems. This was a wonderful, trouble-free arrangement.

Planting Plan: This arrangement was planted with large plants (sizes shown in the photos, left), so it would be full on planting day. One shrimp plant was planted in the center, touching the back. Then, two creeping Jennys were centered on the front rim, angled out. The middle was filled in with five coleus. Other important planting tips are shown on pages 44-45.

Container: International Pottery Alliance's *Scallop Rim Planter* in Oxblood (16" W). Shop for it at www.potteryalliance.com.

Soft Color

1ST

This arrangement rates a blue ribbon (defined on pages 14-17) because it needed absolutely no care at all except water - and it lasted a full, six months in this 15" pot . To get this high performance, be sure to follow the easy planting instructions on pages 44-45.

Tricolor dracaena is combined with Syngonium 'Bold Allusion' and blue peacock fern. This tricolor dracaena centerpiece is similar to the more common dracaena marginata but offers more leaf color. Dracaenas are one of the easiest container plants except for the fact that they drop a lot of leaves.

Tricolor Dracaena
(1 plant from a three-gallon pot)
Plant Profile: Page 151

Syngonium 'Bold Allusion'
(2 plants from 6" pots)
Plant Profile: Page 163

Blue Peacock Fern
(1 plant from a 6" pot)
Plant Profile: Page 167

Cultural Information

Light: Medium to light shade

Season: Spring through fall for most areas. Also thrives in winter in areas where the temperatures stay above 50 degrees. This plant mix takes temperatures from about 50 degrees to the low 100's.

Lifespan: About five to seven months in this container

Both the dracaena and the sygonium grow fairly well indoors. The dracaena is also a popular landscape plant in zones 10-11. Sygonium is quite cold-sensitive, showing leaf browning at about 50 degrees, so it doesn't work in the landscape in most of the world.

Care: Fertilize on planting day with the slow-release mix I describe on page 46. Repeat if the leaves look yellowish or washed-out. That's it! This is a really easy combination unless you place it over pavement, where the frequent leaf droppings will be quite visible.

Water: Water thoroughly when plants show signs of wilt, or the soil feels dry when you push your fingertip into the potting mix (see pages 48-49). I watered this every four days in spring and every two to three days in the heat of summer. It requires less water in medium shade than in light shade. See pages 50-51 to learn about other watering shortcuts.

Troubleshooting: Dracaenas drop a lot of leaves, which could be a problem if you place them over pavement.

Planting Plan: Easy. Plant the dracaena in the middle, along the back edge. Center the fern on the front edge, and add the syngoniums on either side. The container will look full on planting day if you use the plant sizes specified in the photos, left. Be sure to plant in good quality potting <u>mix</u>, not garden soil, top soil, or potting soil, which can kill the plants. Other important planting tips are shown on pages 44-45.

Container: Lotus International #GRS-1524 (15"W x 12"H). They call the color dark red-orange, but it looks brown to me.

Pastels in a Coordinated Pot

Three of my favorite plants - shrimp plant, dragon wing begonia, and torenia - coordinate well with this attractive container. However, the short life of the torenia (three months), coupled with the small size of the container, limit the lifespan of this arrangement to only two to three months. This short lifespan keeps the combo out of the running for any ribbons.

They offer some advantages, however - adapting to a wide range of temperatures and blooming away through the hottest summers or coolest springs. But, be sure to protect them from freezes.

You may find many different kinds of shrimp plants at your garden center - some with red flowers, some a combination of red and yellow. This particular variety (*Pachystatys lutea*) performed best in our trials.

Dragon Wing Begonia
(1 plant from a 6" pot)
Plant Profile: Page 145

Golden Shrimp Plant
(1 plant from a one-gallon pot)
Plant Profile: Page 162

Upright Torenia
(2 plants from 4.5" pots)
Plant Profile: Page 164

Cultural Information

Light: Light shade is ideal. Takes full sun in cooler temperatures.

Season: This plant combination is tolerant of a wide range of temperatures, from mid-40's to the low-100's, which means spring until fall in most areas.

Lifespan: Only two to three months in this small (10" wide) container. The shrimp plant and begonia will last at least six months in a larger container.

Care: Fertilize on planting day with the slow-release mix I describe on page 46. Repeat if the leaves look yellowish or washed out. No trimming is necessary, but the shrimp plant blooms more if the dead flowers are removed.

Water: Water thoroughly when the plants show signs of wilt or the soil feels dry when you push your fingertip into the potting mix (see pages 48-49). I watered this one every day in mid summer and every other day in cooler weather. This plant mix would require less water if planted in a larger container.

Troubleshooting: No problems. This was a wonderful, trouble-free arrangement.

Planting Plan: Plant the shrimp plant in the middle with the torenia on either side. The dragon wing begonia rests in the center, along the front edge of the pot. Be sure to plant in good-quality potting <u>mix</u>, not garden soil, top soil, or potting soil, which can kill the plants. Other important planting tips are shown on pages 44-45.

The arrangement was planted for immediate fullness by dipping the root balls in water to reduce their size. See page 27 to learn this technique.

Container: Global Pottery's *Square Planter* from "The Country Home Collection" (10"H x 10"W) from www.globalpottery.com.

Note about Torenia: Upright torenia lasts about three months. Trailing torenia lasts for up to one year.

Spiky Centerpiece

This arrangement requires nothing but water after it is planted. And the design is foolproof: put a spiky plant in the middle and surround it with smaller plants. However, it misses a blue ribbon because the container is too small to last for the time period required (six months). It would last much longer in a container that has a diameter of at least 14" instead of the 11" pot in the picture. As shown, these plants stay happy in a small container for three to four months.

Many people mistake this ti plant for a dracaena because dracaenas have similar leaves. However, there are many, different ti plants, even though most of them have wider leaves. Ti plants don't drop as much as dracaenas do.

'Florida Sweetheart' Caladium
(2 plants from 4.5" pots)
Plant Profile: Page 147

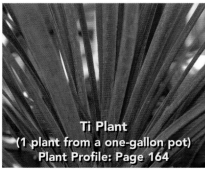

Ti Plant
(1 plant from a one-gallon pot)
Plant Profile: Page 164

Dragon Wing Begonia
(1 plant from a 4.5" pot)
Plant Profile: Page 145

Cultural Information

Light: Light to medium shade

Season: Warm months. Caladiums need temperatures over 65 degrees to do well. This arrangement takes a lot of heat, thriving in temperatures ranging from 65 to over 100 degrees.

Lifespan: The arrangement lasts about three to four months in this container. The ti plant (zone 10-11) can then be transplanted to the garden or into another pot and over-wintered indoors.

Care: Fertilize on planting day with the slow-release mix I describe on page 46. Repeat if the leaves look yellowish or washed-out. No trimming is necessary. Easy!

Water: Water thoroughly when the plants show signs of wilt, or the soil feels dry when you push your fingertip into the potting mix (see pages 48-49). I watered this one every day in mid summer and every other day in cooler weather. This plant mix would require less water if planted in a larger container. See pages 50-51 to learn about other watering shortcuts.

Troubleshooting: No problems. This was a wonderful, trouble-free arrangement. Caladiums are poisonous, however, if eaten.

Planting Plan: A ti plant is placed in the center, touching the back. A dragon wing begonia is planted in the center of the front, with one caladium on either side. I angled all the edge plants out slightly and soaked the root balls in water, so I could squeeze them to reduce their size prior to planting (see page 54). Be sure to plant in good-quality potting mix, not garden soil, top soil, or potting soil, which can kill the plants. Other important planting tips are shown on pages 44-45.

Container: Global Pottery *Daisy Planter* in white (12"H x 11"W). Go to www.globalpottery.com for sources.

Note: Be sure to plant dwarf caladiums instead of larger ones in an arrangements such as this, so they don't outgrow the centerpiece.

Shade Color

A 'Gemini' anthurium forms the centerpiece of this easy, long-lasting, shade arrangement. This combination rates a blue ribbon (defined on pages 14-17) because it requires no care other than water after planting and lasts for five to six months. To get this high performance, be sure to follow the easy planting instructions on pages 44-45.

The pink color of the anthurium flower is repeated in the leaves of the red Ann fittonia, which I found in the house plant section of a garden center. The bromeliads mark the center of the arrangement and blend well with the other plantings.

Red Ann Fittonia
(2 plants from 5" pots)
Plant Profile: Page 169

Anthurium 'Gemini'
(1 plant from a 6" pot)
Plant Profile: Page 145

Bromeliad
(1 plant from a 6" pot)
Plant Profile: Page 146

Cultural Information

Light: Medium shade. Anthuriums burn in any sun at all.

Season: Plant when the temperatures range from 50 to 95 degrees. I haven't tried them in temperatures higher than that.

Lifespan: Five to six months in this container. Anthuriums and bromeliads last longer than most plants in containers this small.

Care: Fertilize on planting day with the slow-release mix I describe on page 46. Repeat if the leaves look yellowish or washed-out. No trimming is necessary. Easy!

Water: Water thoroughly when the plants show signs of wilt, or the soil feels dry when you push your fingertip into the potting mix (see pages 48-49). I watered this once a week in spring and twice a week in summer. See pages 50-51 to learn about watering shortcuts.

Troubleshooting: No problems. This was a wonderful, trouble-free arrangement.

Planting Plan: Easy. Plant the anthurium in the middle and the bromeliads along the front edge. Surround them with the fittonia. Be sure to plant in good-quality potting <u>mix</u>, not garden soil, top soil, or potting soil, which can kill the plants.

Container: Global Pottery's *Oval Fleur de Lis* in Tuscan green (16"W x 11"D x 9"H). Shop for it at www.globalpottery.com.

Note: One of my readers' most frequent questions is what to plant in deep shade. Anthuriums are one of the few plants that will bloom with that little light. And, they are very easy to grow in most areas in the summer. I haven't had much luck with them indoors, however.

I classed this arrangement as medium shade because the bromeliads will lose their pink leaf color in dense shade.

Easy and Beautiful!

This gorgeous arrangement was very easy to care for and lasted six months. It rated a red ribbon (defined on pages 18-19) instead of a blue because New Guinea impatiens are somewhat susceptible to pests. However, I didn't do anything to this arrangement after planting other than add water. To get this high performance, be sure to follow the easy planting instructions on pages 44-45.

The handcrafted iron container combines unique container material with a terrific contemporary design that resembles sculpture. It comes in either a natural rust or powder coat finish. We tested the natural rust and are thrilled with its appearance after eighteen months outside. During its five-to-ten year lifespan, it continues to oxidize, becoming quite rustic in appearance.

New Guinea Impatiens 'Infinity Orange'
(4 plants from 4.5" pots)
Plant Profile: Page 154

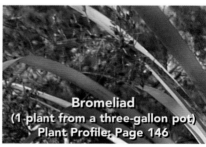

Bromeliad
(1 plant from a three-gallon pot)
Plant Profile: Page 146

New Guinea Impatiens, 'Infinity Dark Pink'
(4 plants from 4.5" pots)
Plant Profile: Page 154

Cultural Information

Light: Light to medium shade

Season: Grow this arrangement in temperatures ranging from 40 to 95 degrees. New Guinea impatiens will live in higher temperatures but not flower well.

Lifespan: Five to six months in this container. New Guinea impatiens are at the end of their lifespan at that point. Bromeliads live for about 2 years but send up babies to replace themselves provided they are protected from frost. The bromeliad flower lasts about three to four months. However, the New Guinea impatiens add so much color that the bromeliad flower is hardly missed!

Care: Fertilize on planting day with the slow-release mix I describe on page 46. Repeat every 6 months. Put the fertilizer in the potting mix around the plants, not in the center cup.

Water: Bromeliads and impatiens seem like unlikely companions because of their differences in water needs. Bromeliads will live on weekly watering, whereas impatiens require more. However, many bromeliads are native to rain forests, which are accustomed to wet and dry seasons. They exist quite happily with the same amount of water that thirsty impatiens crave.

Water thoroughly when the plants show signs of wilt, or the soil feels dry when you push your fingertip into the potting mix. I watered this twice a week in spring and every other day in summer. Water the potting mix instead of the center well of the bromeliad.

Troubleshooting: Some bromeliads, these included, have sharp spines.

Planting Plan: Easy. Plant the large bromeliad in the center, and surround it with the impatiens. Other important planting tips are shown on pages 44-45.

Container: Ore #112 *Urn*, (28"W x 28"D x 12"H) on a #106 *Column* (12"W x 32"H). Shop for it at www.orecontainers.com.

Easy Plants in a Gorgeous Pot

This arrangement rated a red ribbon (defined on pages 18-19) instead of a blue because New Guinea impatiens are somewhat susceptible to pests. However, I didn't do anything to this arrangement after planting other than add water. And it lasted for an entire six months in this large container. To get this high performance, be sure to follow the easy planting instructions on pages 44-45.

Although the bromeliad didn't flower for the full six months, the impatiens did so well they took up the slack when the bromeliad wasn't blooming.

The container is made of fiberglass, which is long-lasting and easy to clean.

New Guinea Impatiens, 'Infinity Dark Pink' (4 plants from 6" pots) Plant Profile: Page 154

Bromeliad (1 plant from a one-gallon pot) Plant Profile: Page 146

New Guinea Impatiens, 'Infinity Orange' (3 plants from 6" pots) Plant Profile: Page 154

Cultural Information

Light: In most of the world, bromeliads are sold in the house plant section of your local garden centers. Because they are grown in very low light, the leaves burn in any sun at all. Keep them in medium shade, which suits the impatiens as well.

However, garden centers in subtropical areas (like parts of Florida and California) frequently sell bromeliads that are adapted to higher light. Ask at your garden center if you see one you would like to use in more light.

Season: Any time the temperatures are over 40 and under 100 degrees. New Guinea impatiens take more heat than regular impatiens, but bloom more when temperatures are under 93 degrees.

Lifespan: Bromeliads last indefinitely, if occasionally separated and protected from frost. However, many gardeners looking for easy impact keep the bromeliad for the two to four month bloom period and then discard it. New Guinea impatiens last about five to six months in a container this large.

Care: Easy! No trimming necessary. Fertilize on planting day with the slow-release mix I describe on page 46. Repeat every 6 months. Put the fertilizer in the potting mix around the plants, not in the center cup.

Water: Water thoroughly when the soil feels dry to the touch, or the impatiens show signs of wilt. This arrangement needs water about every three to five days in medium shade.

Troubleshooting: No problems. This was a wonderful, trouble-free arrangement. New Guinea impatiens get can get fungus occasionally, however.

Planting Plan: Plant the bromeliad in the center, and surround it with the impatiens.

Container: Campania's Fiberglass Collection, *Round Leaf Planter* (22"W x 14.25"H) on *Square Frame Pedestal* (16"W x 21"H). Go to www.campaniainternational.com for sources.

Inspiration From a Fish!

I chose the colors of the plants in this arrangement from the fish, a piece of Mexican pottery. New Guinea impatiens form the centerpiece, accented by blue lobelia and lime creeping Jenny. Lobelia is a very popular container plant, but I have had inconsistent results with it. The primary problem is it doesn't last an entire season and blooms intermittently. It is so beautiful, however, that I will keep trying!

Using plants with different sizes of flowers work well in most arrangements, as shown here with the large, New Guinea impatiens contrasted with the small lobelia flowers.

This arrangement missed a ribbon because of the erratic performance of lobelia.

New Guinea Impatiens
2 plants from 6" pots
Plant Profile: Page 154

Creeping Jenny
4 plants from 4.5" pots
Plant Profile: Page 149

Lobelia
2 plants from 4.5" pots
Plant Profile: Page 168

Cultural Information

Light: Light shade

Season: When the temperatures are over 40 and under 90 degrees.

Lifespan: About three months. New Guinea impatiens and creeping Jenny last longer, but that is the maximum amount of time lobelia has bloomed for me. In an arrangement that looks this good, it makes sense to simply replace the lobelia with another plant if it dies first. See page 52 to learn how to do it.

Care: Easy! No trimming necessary. Fertilize on planting day with the slow-release mix I describe on page 46.

However, the impatiens drop a lot of hard-to-remove flowers if placed on a deck, as shown here.

Water: Water thoroughly when the soil feels dry to the touch, or the impatiens show signs of wilt (see pages 48-49). This arrangement needs water about every two to four days in light shade. See pages 50-51 to learn about watering shortcuts.

Troubleshooting: The lobelia didn't live as long as the other plants. Also, New Guinea impatiens get can get fungus occasionally.

Planting Plan: Plant the impatiens along the back rim of the pot, centered. Plant the lobelia centered along the front edge, angled out. Fill in with the creeping Jenny. Be sure to plant in good-quality potting <u>mix</u>, not garden soil, top soil, or potting soil, which can kill your plants. Other important planting tips are shown on pages 44-45.

Container: International Pottery Alliance's *Scallop Rim Planter* in Oxblood (14" W). Shop for it at www.potteryalliance.com.

Fish: Shop for the fish at www.masart.com.

Color that Likes It Hot

1ST

Pink and grey combine to make an attractive but tough, heat-tolerant combination in this blue ribbon arrangement. It required nothing but water during its entire six month lifespan. To get this high performance, be sure to follow the easy planting instructions on pages 44-45.

This was our first experience with silver licorice plant and I was quite thrilled that it breezed through our hot summer.

This pot is lightweight fiberglass, so I was able to carry it around a nursery in search of plants that looked good with it. Fiberglass is an excellent container material. It is durable (think about it - boats are made of fiberglass!), easy to clean, and available in attractive finishes, like this grey one.

Diplademia
(1 plant from a three-gallon pot)
Plant Profile: Page 151

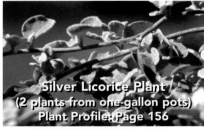

Silver Licorice Plant
(2 plants from one-gallon pots)
Plant Profile: Page 156

'Florida Sweetheart' Caladium
(4 plants from 4.5" pots)
Plant Profile: Page 147

Cultural Information

Light: Full sun to light shade

Season: Spring and summer in areas where temperatures range from 65 to over 100 degrees.

Lifespan: This arrangement is happy in this size pot for about five to six months. Be sure that the caladiums are dwarfs, or they will quickly outgrow the diplademia.

Although diplademia is classed as a perennial, I have never had much luck with it living more than one season in the ground - even in zone 10 - where it is supposed to thrive. Use it as an annual.

Care: Easy! No trimming necessary. Fertilize on planting day with the slow-release mix I describe on page 46.

Water: Water thoroughly when the plants show signs of wilt, or the soil feels dry when you push your fingertip into the potting mix (see pages 48-49). I watered this twice a week in spring and every day in summer. See pages 50-51 to learn about watering shortcuts.

Troubleshooting: The paint chipped off the pot after three years. If this happens to you, take it to your local paint store so they can match up the color. Touch up the paint following the manufacturer's instructions.

The diplademia went out of bloom but only for a very short time.

Caladiums are poisonous.

Planting Plan: Plant the diplademia along the back edge, centered. Plant the caladium along the front edge, surrounded by the silver licorice plant. Be sure to plant in good-quality potting <u>mix</u>, not garden soil, top soil, or potting soil, which can kill the plants. Other important planting tips are shown on pages 44-45.

Container: Global Pottery *Venice Urn* in lead from their Fiberglass Collection (21"W x 18.5"H). Shop for it at www.globalpottery.com.

Easy Pansies

Here's a cool-season combination that is simple to plant; it lasts for six months in most areas, easily rating a blue ribbon. To get this high performance, be sure to follow the easy planting instructions on pages 44-45.

Pansies are one of the stars of easy container gardening. They bloom in cool weather, which causes them to grow slowly. The slow growth means they can stay in smaller containers for longer periods of time than most other flowers.

Make more impact by using several related containers together, as shown, right.

Blue Pansy
(6 plants from 4" pots)
Plant Profile: Page 158

Sedum
(8 plants from 4" pots)
Plant Profile: Page 162

Orange Pansy
(6 plants from 4" pots)
Plant Profile: Page 158

Cultural Information

Light: Light shade to full sun

Season: Cool season when temperatures range from 22 to 85 degrees. Shows some cold damage below 25 degrees, but recovers quickly. I have had pansies in containers in temperatures down to 15 degrees. They look bad when the weather gets that cold, but they recover quickly when it warms up. If you want them to look good all winter, bring them inside if the temperatures drop below 25 degrees.

Pansies are commonly used in the spring and fall in areas that have bitterly cold winters.

Lifespan: Six months in this container

Care: Easy! No trimming necessary. Fertilize on planting day with the slow-release mix I describe on page 46.

If you have time, pinch off the dead pansy flowers.

Water: Water thoroughly when the plants show signs of wilt or the soil feels dry when you push your fingertip into the potting mix (see pages 48-49). See pages 50-51 to learn about watering shortcuts.

As long as it rains occasionally, you shouldn't need to water much during cool weather. Conversely, very cold weather dries soil out, so be sure to water before a really cold spell arrives.

Troubleshooting: No problems at all

Planting Plan: Plant the blue pansies in a line along the center in a line Plant the orange pansies in a line perpendicular to the blues. Fill in along the edges with the sedum. Be sure to plant in good quality potting <u>mix</u>, not garden soil, top soil, or potting soil, which can kill the plants.

Container: 16" bowl

Photos from Gibbs Gardens in Ball Ground, Georgia

Chapter 5

Four (or More) Plant Combos

Planting four or more plants in a container is obviously more complicated than just one or two. But, it is a lot of fun to fill your shopping cart with gorgeous plants that look great together. Here are some tips:

✿ Be sure to choose plants that like the same growing conditions.

✿ Vary leaf and flower size. Combine large leaves or flowers with tiny leaves or flowers.

✿ Vary leaf and flower shape. Combine round leaves or flowers with spiky leaves or flowers.

Above and left: Tall snapdragons form the centerpieces of both these containers. They look great when all the flowers bloom at once. One caution: The snapdragons all stop blooming at the same time while new buds are forming. The flowers re-appear in about a month later. This factor causes them to miss a ribbon.

The hanging basket is so large that it still looks great without the snapdragon flowers. It lasted about six months during 40 to 85 degree temperatures.

The bowl was planted with large plants shortly before this photo was taken. The plants were so large compared with the size of the pot that the arrangement only lasted about six weeks. But the low cost, coupled with the ease of planting made it well worth the time and money.

The Drama of Black

What luck! I found a black and lime green pot to go with these plants in the same colors. This combination was a favorite of many visitors to my garden. It misses a ribbon, however, because the sweet potato vine grows like Jack-and-the-Beanstalk and attracts lots of bugs.

It lasted a full six months. I let the sweet potato grow all over the deck, and it looked terrific!

Proven Winners provided the plants for this arrangement.

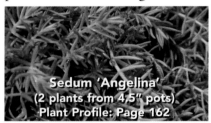

Sedum 'Angelina'
(2 plants from 4.5" pots)
Plant Profile: Page 162

Elephant Ear
(1 plant from a one-gallon pot)
Plant Profile: Page 157

'Margarita' Sweet Potato
(2 plants from 4.5" pots)
Plant Profile: Page 163

'Black Heart' Sweet Potato
(2 plants from 4.5" pots)
Plant Profile: Page 163

'Gay's Delight' Coleus
(2 plants from 4.5" pots)
Plant Profile: Page 148

Cultural Information

Light: Full sun to light shade

Season: Whenever temperatures range from 40 degrees to the low 100's.

Lifespan: About six months in this large container

Care: Trim the sweet potato to keep it in check. If the temperatures are over 90 degrees, expect to trim it monthly. Fertilize on planting day with the slow-release mix I describe on page 46.

Water: Water thoroughly when the plants show signs of wilt, or the soil feels dry when you push your fingertip into the potting mix (see pages 48-49). I watered this twice a week in spring and every day in summer. See pages 50-51 to learn about watering shortcuts.

Troubleshooting: Sweet potato plants are frequently bothered by pests. Some eat tiny holes in the leaves, which I leave alone because they don't show much. Others, like snails, slugs, and Japanese beetles, almost devour the leaves. If yours get attacked, ask you garden center for the least toxic spray. Avoid Japanese beetle bait traps; as they attract more beetles than they kill.

Planting Plan: Plant the elephant ear in the center, with the sweet potato vines on either side. Fill in with the sedum and coleus. Be sure to plant in good-quality potting mix, not garden soil, top soil, or potting soil, which can kill the plants. Other important planting tips are shown on pages 44-45.

Container: International Pottery Alliance, Marco Polo Collection, *Olive Jar* (20" W) in 'Tropical Yellow' (I call it black and lime green!). Shop for it at www.potteryalliance.com.

Silvers!

Silvers are hot! Entire plant books are devoted to this unique leaf and flower color. This arrangement, from a private garden in Philadelphia, combines different silvers perfectly. It doesn't rate a ribbon because not all of the plants last for at least six months. But, what a beauty!

Notice how well the large leaves of the succulents and rex begonias contrast with the tiny leaves of the dicondra 'Silver Falls.'

Echeveria spp.
(1 plant from a 4"pot)
Plant Profile: Page 151

Begonia, Rex
(1 plant from a 6" pot)
Plant Profile: Page 166

Dicondra 'Silver Falls'
(6 plants from 4" pots)
Plant Profile: Page 148

Begonia, Rex
(1 plant from a 6" pot)
Plant Profile: Page 166

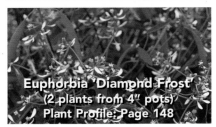

Euphorbia 'Diamond Frost'
(2 plants from 4" pots)
Plant Profile: Page 148

Cultural Information

Light: Light shade

Season: Plant when temperatures range from 50 to 85 degrees.

Lifespan: This arrangement is happy in this size pot for about three to four months.

Care: Trim the dicondra when it reaches the ground. Fertilize on planting day with the slow-release mix I describe on page 46.

Water: Water thoroughly when the plants show signs of wilt, or the soil feels dry when you push your fingertip into the potting mix (see pages 48-49). See pages 50-51 to learn about watering shortcuts.

Troubleshooting: No problems

Planting Plan: Plant the begonias, echeveria, and 'Diamond Frost' in the center. Tuck in the dicondra along the edge.

Container: Concrete trough (about 28"L x 10"W x 10"T)

Textural Mix

2ND

This arrangement rates a red ribbon (defined on pages 18-19) instead of a blue because it requires one additional chore other than watering: monthly trimming, which only takes about five minutes! However, this plant mix lasts at least the five-to-six month red ribbon minimum in this large container, and the arrangement was trouble free. Be sure to follow the easy planting instructions on pages 44-45.

Each plant in this arrangement is quite different in texture, which is as important as color in mixed plantings. Most of the plants are from Proven Winners.

Curly Copperleaf
(1 plant from a one-gallon pot)
Plant Profile: Page 149

Carex 'Frosty Curls'
(2 plants from 4.5" pots)
Plant Profile: Page 154

Coleus 'Crime Scene'
(2 plants from 4.5" pots)
Plant Profile: Page 148

Creeping Jenny
(2 plants from one-gallon pots)
Plant Profile: Page 149

Cultural Information

Light: Full sun to light shade

Season: Anytime the temperatures range between 45 degrees and the low 100's.

Lifespan: The arrangement lasts about six months in this 16 inch pot. Plant the copperleaf in your garden after the other plants die if you live in zones 10-11.

Care: Pinch back the coleus every month or so. Trim the tips off the copperleaf if it starts looking a bit leggy. Trim the bottom of the creeping Jenny before it starts to touch the ground. Fertilize on planting day with the slow-release mix I describe on page 46.

Water: Water thoroughly when the plants show signs of wilt, or the soil feels dry when you push your fingertip into the potting mix (see pages 48-49). I watered this twice a week in spring and every day in summer. See pages 50-51 to learn about watering shortcuts.

Troubleshooting: No problems

Planting Plan: Plant the copperleaf along the back edge, centered. Plant the coleus along the front edge, surrounded by the grasses. Tuck in the creeping Jenny plants on either side. Be sure to plant in good-quality potting <u>mix</u>, not garden soil, top soil, or potting soil, which can kill the plants. Other important planting tips are shown on pages 44-45.

Container: International Pottery Alliance, Old World Terracotta Collection, *Rippled Egg Pot*, 16" W.

Shop for it at www.potteryalliance.com.

Ideal for Pools and Patios

Bright-colored plants don't have to make a mess! All of these plants are ideal for pool decks because they give continuous color without dropping a lot of debris. This arrangement misses a ribbon, however, because the sweet potato vine grows like Jack-and-the-Beanstalk and attracts lots of bugs.

This colorful combo lasted a full six months in this large pot that measures a full 21 inches across. I let the sweet potato grow all over the deck, and it looked terrific!

'Madame Chaoul' Ti Plant
(1 plant from a three-gallon pot)
Plant Profile: Page 164

Golden Shrimp Plant
(2 plants from one-gallon pots)
Plant Profile: Page 162

Mammey Croton
(2 plants from one-gallon pots)
Plant Profile: Page 149

Margarita Sweet Potato
(4 plants from 4" pots)
Plant Profile: Page 163

Cultural Information

Light: Full sun to medium shade. If the temperatures reach as high as the mid-90's, stick to light shade.

Season: Anytime temperatures range from 45 degrees to the low 100's. These plants are happy in either extreme.

Lifespan: About six months in this container. All of the plants (except the sweet potato vine) last for years in frost-free locations. If you live in a frost-free area, move them into larger pots or into your frost-free garden when they outgrow this one.

Care: Trim the vines so they don't take over the arrangement. Fertilize on planting day with the slow-release mix I describe on page 46.

Water: Water thoroughly when the plants show signs of wilt, or the soil feels dry when you push your fingertip into the potting mix (see pages 48-49). I watered this twice a week in spring and every day in summer. See pages 50-51 to learn about watering shortcuts.

Troubleshooting: Sweet potato plants are frequently bothered by pests. Some eat tiny holes in the leaves, and I leave these alone because they don't show much. Others, like snails, slugs, and Japanese beetles, almost devour the leaves. If yours get attacked, ask you garden center for the least toxic spray. Avoid Japanese beetle bait traps; they attract more beetles than they kill.

Planting Plan: Plant the ti plant in the center with the mammey crotons planted directly in front of it. Plant shrimp plants on either side of the crotons, with a sweet potato vine in front, trailing over the edge. Be sure to plant in good-quality potting mix, not garden soil, top soil, or potting soil, which can kill the plants. Other important planting tips are shown on pages 44-45.

Container: International Pottery Alliance's *Rolled Rim Planter* from their *Marco Polo Collection*. Saddle red. 20" W. Shop for it at www.potteryalliance.com.

Chapter 6

Side-Planted Containers
(Video demonstrations at www.sideplanting.com)

Video Series, Part 1: What is Side Planting?
(3 minutes)

Video Series, Part 2: Planting
(3 minutes)

Video Series, Part 4: Fertilization and Trimming
(1.5 Minutes)

Video Series, Part 5: Wall Baskets and
Window Boxes (2.5 Minutes)

Video Series, Part 3: Container Care and Watering (3 minutes)

Video Series, Part 6: Patio Stands and Border Columns (3.5 Minutes)

Side-planted containers are planted in the sides as well as in the top of the containers. This technique offers instant fullness and long-lasting results. See pages 40-43 of this book for more information.

This unique container system also offers columns and stands that bring the plants closer to eye level.

I made a video series of six demonstrations, none over three minutes long. This series is ideal for learning about this new, revolutionary container technique.

Go to www.sideplanting.com to see the videos as well as other technical information.

I also wrote a book called "Instant Container Gardens" that is totally devoted to side-planting. It features completely different container profiles than this book. It also shows you how to transform your garden with these unique containers.

Above: This photo shows a 16" basket on a stand (all in one combo) empty and planted. The planted basket is only two weeks old!

Pink and Purple

36" window box

This arrangement rates a red ribbon instead of a blue because the cleome went out of bloom a few times. But, it looked fabulous for a full six months, requiring nothing but water the entire time! To get this high performance, be sure to follow the easy planting instructions on pages 42-43.

Planting Sequence

Step 1: Alternate the begonias and the scaevola around the side layer.

Step 2: Plant the cleomes in the center, surrounded by the angelonia.

Step 3: Repeat Step 1 around the edge. Be sure to put different plants above each other. *(For full planting demo, see pages 42-43.)*

Cultural Information

Light: Full sun to light shade

Season: Plant when the temperatures range from 45 degrees to the low 100's. This arrangement tolerates both extremes well.

Lifespan: Five to six months in this large, 36" window box

Care: Fertilize on planting day with the slow-release mix I describe on page 46. Repeat if the leaves look yellowish or washed out. Trim the scaevola if it gets too long. For my three minute trimming video, see *Fertilization and Trimming* at www.sideplanting.com.

Water: Water thoroughly when plants show signs of wilt, or the soil feels dry when you push your fingertip into the potting mix (see pages 48-49). I watered this every three days in spring and every day in the heat of summer.

Troubleshooting: No problems. This was a wonderful, trouble-free arrangement.

Planting Plan: This arrangement was planted with large plants (sizes shown in the photos, left), so it would be full on planting day. See the "Planting Sequence", left. Other important planting tips are shown on pages 42-43.

Container: Kinsman's #CLZW36 window box (36"L x 9"W x 9"D). Go to www.sideplanting.com to find a list of garden center sources near you. To purchase by phone, call 1-800-733-4146 for retail orders or 1-800-733-5613 for wholesale orders.

To purchase online, go to www.kinsmangarden.com for retail and www.kinsmanwholesale.com for wholesale.

Hanging the Window Box: It's easy! See the video demo at www.sideplanting.com.

For 3-minute planting video, go to www.sideplanting.com

Just one week after planting!

Wax Begonia, Pink
(6 plants from 4" pots)
Plant profile: Page 145

Serena Angelonia
(4 plants from 4" pots)
Plant profile: Page 144

Cleome
(3 plants from 6" pots)
Plant profile: Page 166

Scaevola
(6 plants from 4" pots)
Plant profile: Page 161

Wax Begonia, White
(6 plants from 4" pots)
Plant profile: Page 145

36" window box

Weekly Water Only!

This blue ribbon arrangement has everything - it looks great and required nothing but water for its full, seven-month lifespan! Since the container is large and was placed in shade, it only needed water once a week from April until July! I watered twice a week in July and August and then back to once a week from September to November.

Planting Sequence

Step 1: Alternate the begonias and creeping Jenny around the side layer.

Step 2: Plant the ti plant in the center, surrounded by the coleus.

Step 3: Repeat Step 1 around the edge. Be sure to put different plants above each other. (*This window box was planted with smaller plants than the one on the previous page. It took about three weeks longer for it to fill in completely.*)

Cultural Information

Light: Light to medium shade

Season: Plant when the temperatures range from 45 degrees to the low 100's. This arrangement tolerates both extremes well.

Lifespan: Six to seven months in this large, 36" window box

Care: As easy as it gets! Fertilize on planting day with the slow-release mix I describe on page 46. Repeat if the leaves look yellowish or washed out. That's it! No trimming required unless the creeping Jenny hits the ground.

Water: Water thoroughly when plants show signs of wilt, or the soil feels dry when you push your fingertip into the potting mix (see pages 48-49). I watered this once a week in spring and twice a week in the heat of summer.

Troubleshooting: No problems. This was a wonderful, trouble-free arrangement.

Planting Plan: See the "Planting Sequence," left. Other important planting tips are shown on pages 42-43.

Container: Kinsman's #CLZW36 window box (36"L x 9"W x 9"D). Go to www.sideplanting.com to find a list of garden center sources near you. To purchase by phone, call 1-800-733-4146 for retail orders or 1-800-733-5613 for wholesale orders.

To purchase online, go to www.kinsmangarden.com for retail and www.kinsmanwholesale.com for wholesale.

Hanging the Window Box: It's easy! See the video demo at www.sideplanting.com.

Note on Heat Tolerance: This plant combination is excellent for adapting to temperature extremes. It thrives in temperatures as low as 45 degrees and up to the low 100's. It breezed through a ten day run of over 100 degrees, only requiring water twice a week during that record-breaking heat wave.

For 3-minute planting video, go to www.sideplanting.com

Begonia 'Cherry Blossom'
(9 plants from 3" pots)
Plant Profile: Page 166

Ti Plant
(1 plant from a one-gallon pot)
Plant Profile: Page 164

Coleus 'Kong Rose'
(2 plants from 6" pots)
Plant Profile: Page 150

Creeping Jenny
(9 plants from 3" pots)
Plant Profile: Page 149

Useful Wall Pot

16" wall basket

Wall pots are great for entries, decks, trellises, or columns. And, they are light enough to stay put with just two screws. This one is too small, however, to support the plants for a full six months, so it doesn't get a ribbon. But, it will give you a good three months beauty with very little care.

The design is quite simple, with a ti plant in the middle and coleus alternated around the sides and edge.

Ti Plant
(1 plant from a one-gallon pot)
Plant Profile: Page 164

Coleus, Unnamed
(4 plants from 4.5" pots)
Plant Profile: Page 148

Coleus, Unnamed
(4 plants from 4.5" pots)
Plant Profile: Page 148

Coleus, Unnamed
(4 plants from 4.5" pots)
Plant Profile: Page 148

Cultural Information

Light: Medium shade to full sun

Season: Plant when the temperatures range from 45 degrees to the low 100's. This arrangement tolerates both extremes well.

Lifespan: About three months in this small, wall pot

Care: Fertilize on planting day with the slow-release mix I describe on page 46. Repeat if the leaves look yellowish or washed out. Pinch back the coleus monthly.

Water: Water thoroughly when plants show signs of wilt, or the soil feels dry when you push your fingertip into the potting mix (see pages 48-49). Expect to water every day.

Troubleshooting: No problems. This was a wonderful, trouble-free arrangement.

Planting Plan: Alternate the three coleus around the sides. Plant the ti plant in the center. Alternate the three coleus around the edge.

Container: Kinsman's #CLZH16 wall pot (16"L x 8"W x 7"D). Go to www.sideplanting.com to find a list of garden center sources near you. To purchase by phone, call 1-800-733-4146 for retail orders or 1-800-733-5613 for wholesale orders.

To purchase online, go to www.kinsmangarden.com for retail and www.kinsmanwholesale.com for wholesale.

Hanging the Wall Pot: It's easy! See the video demo at www.sideplanting.com.

For 3-minute planting video, go to www.sideplanting.com

1ST Easy and Long-lived

I was amazed at the performance of these plants in a long, hot summer. They bloomed continuously through seven months of record-breaking temperatures, including a ten day run of temperatures over 100 degrees! I did nothing to any of them other than water for their entire, seven month life! To get this high performance, be sure to follow the easy planting instructions on pages 42-43.

The centerpiece (*Salvia farinacea* 'Mystic Spires') is the best salvia I have ever tried in containers. It lasted a full seven months without growing so large that it might fall over or take over the arrangement.

Salvia farinacea 'Mystic Spires'
(3 plants from 4" pots)
Plant Profile: Page 161

Creeping Jenny
(18 plants from 4" pots)
Plant Profile: Page 149

Scaevola 'New Blue Wonder'
(17 plants from 4" pots)
Plant Profile: Page 161

Cultural Information

Light: Medium shade to full sun

Season: Plant when the temperatures range from 45 degrees to the low 100's. This arrangement tolerates both extremes well.

Lifespan: About seven months in this large container

Care: Fertilize on planting day with the slow-release mix I describe on page 46. Repeat if the leaves look yellowish or washed out. If you have time, remove the dead flowers from the salvia.

Water: Water thoroughly when plants show signs of wilt, or the soil feels dry when you push your fingertip into the potting mix (see pages 48-49). Expect to water every day in summer. This container is a great candidate for an automatic drip irrigation system (page 51). If attached to a timer, you never have to spend time watering.

Troubleshooting: No problems

Planting Plan: Alternate creeping Jenny and scaevola around the sides. Plant the salvia in the center. Alternate the creeping Jenny and scaevola again around the edge.

Container: Kinsman's #ZGB20 double basket (20"W x 11"D). Go to www.sideplanting.com to find a list of garden center sources near you. To purchase by phone, call 1-800-733-4146 for retail orders or 1-800-733-5613 for wholesale orders. To purchase online: www.kinsmangarden.com for retail and www.kinsmanwholesale.com for wholesale.

Installing the Column: The 42" column is sold in a kit that installs easily and fits this basket well. The product number is ZGBC42. Shop for it at Kinsman Company (contact info under "Container," above). To see a 3.5 minute video of its installation, go to www.sideplanting.com and watch Part 6, *Patio Stands an Border Columns.*

For 3-minute planting video, go to www.sideplanting.com

Easy and Beautiful!

20" double basic basket

This gorgeous arrangement was almost trouble free. However, since Japanese beetles attacked the sweet potato vines, it misses a ribbon. Other than spraying once, I did nothing to this other than add water! The 'Sweet Caroline' sweet potato didn't take over the container, which has happened with other varieties.

Planting Sequence

Step 1: In the side layer, alternate the sweet potato, silver licorice, and begonia.

Step 2: Repeat step 1 on the next layer.

Step 3: Plant the ti plants in the middle.

Step 4: Plant the edge plants in the same pattern as the first two steps.

Cultural Information

Light: Light shade to full sun

Season: Plant when the temperatures range from 45 degrees to the low 100's. This arrangement tolerates both extremes well.

Lifespan: About seven months in this large container

Care: Fertilize on planting day with the slow-release mix I describe on page 46. Repeat if the leaves look yellowish or washed out.

Water: Water thoroughly when plants show signs of wilt, or the soil feels dry when you push your fingertip into the potting mix (see pages 48-49). Expect to water every day in summer. This container is a great candidate for an automatic drip irrigation system (page 51).

Troubleshooting: Sweet potato plants are frequently bothered by pests. Some eat tiny holes in the leaves, which I leave alone because they don't show much. Others, like snails, slugs, and Japanese beetles, almost devour the leaves. If yours get attacked, ask your garden center for the least toxic spray. Avoid Japanese beetle bait traps, as they attract more beetles than they kill.

Planting Plan: See "Planting Sequence," left

Container: Kinsman's #ZGBD20 double basket (20"W x 11"D). Go to www.sideplanting.com to find a list of garden center sources near you. To purchase by phone, call 1-800-733-4146 for retail orders or 1-800-733-5613 for wholesale orders. To purchase online: www.kinsmangarden.com for retail and www.kinsmanwholesale.com for wholesale.

Installing the Column: The 42" column is sold in a kit that installs easily and fits this planter well. The product number is ZGBC42. Shop for it at Kinsman Company (contact info under "Container," above). To see a 3.5 minute video of its installation, go to www.sideplanting.com and watch Part 6, *Patio Stands and Border Columns.*

For 3-minute planting video, go to www.sideplanting.com

Ti Plant
(3 plants from 6" pots)
Plant Profile: Page 164

Silver Licorice Plant
(12 plants from 4" pots)
Plant Profile: Page 156

'Sweet Caroline'
Sweet Potato
(12 plants from 4" pots)
Plant Profile: Page 163

Dragon Wing Begonia
(11 plants from 4" pots)
Plant Profile: Page 145

Thrived for Seven Months

16" single basic basket

I was thrilled with the performance of this arrangement. Other than spraying the sweet potato vine once for bugs, I didn't do anything other than watering for seven months, even during a record-breaking heat wave. The 'Sweet Caroline' sweet potato behaved much better than many of the other varieties I have tried.

The blanket petunias bloomed the whole time, longer than any other petunia in our trials. They slowed down occasionally, but the 'Chocolate Drop' coleus took up the slack.

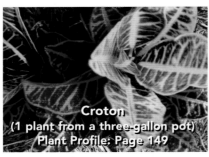

Croton
(1 plant from a three-gallon pot)
Plant Profile: Page 149

Blanket Petunia
(8 plants from 4" pots)
Plant Profile: Page 160

Coleus 'Chocolate Drop'
(8 plants from 4" pots)
Plant Profile: Page 148

**'Sweet Caroline'
Sweet Potato**
(8 plants from 4" pots)
Plant Profile: Page 163

Cultural Information

Light: Light shade to full sun

Season: Plant when the temperatures range from 45 degrees to the low 100's. This arrangement tolerates both extremes well.

Lifespan: About seven months in this large container

Care: Fertilize on planting day with the slow-release mix I describe on page 46. Repeat if the leaves look yellowish or washed out. Trim the sweet potato if it gets too long.

Water: Water thoroughly when plants show signs of wilt, or the soil feels dry when you push your fingertip into the potting mix (see pages 48-49). Expect to water every day in summer. This container is a great candidate for an automatic drip irrigation system (page 51).

Troubleshooting: Sweet potato plants are frequently bothered by pests. Some eat tiny holes in the leaves, which I leave alone because they don't show much. Others, like snails, slugs, and Japanese beetles, almost devour the leaves. If yours get attacked, ask your garden center for the least toxic spray. Avoid Japanese beetle bait traps, as they attract more beetles than they kill.

Planting Plan: Alternate the petunias, coleus, and sweet potatoes in the side holes. Plant the croton in the center. Alternate the smaller plants again around the edge.

Container: Kinsman's #ZGBS16 single basket (16"W x 7"D). Go to www.sideplanting.com to find a list of garden center sources near you. To purchase by phone, call 1-800-733-4146 for retail orders or 1-800-733-5613 for wholesale orders. To purchase online: www.kinsmangarden.com for retail and www.kinsmanwholesale.com for wholesale.

Installing the Column: The 36" column is sold in a kit that installs easily and fits this planter well. The product number is ZGBC36. Shop for it at Kinsman Company (contact info under "Container," above). To see a 3.5 minute video of its installation, go to www.sideplanting.com and watch Part 6, *Patio Stands and Border Columns.*

For 3-minute planting video, go to www.sideplanting.com

Pink, Purple, and Silver

16" double basic basket

This arrangement is one of the most beautiful I have ever planted. It only lasted about three months, however, because the iresine and calibrachoa reached the end of their lifespan. I don't know if their early demise was attributable to the high temperatures they encountered in July, or they naturally live for only three months.

Both the Persian shield and glamourous dicondra 'Silver Falls' are blue ribbon plants, that last at least six months.

Persian Shield
(1 plant from a one-gallon pot)
Plant Profile: Page 159

Dicondra 'Silver Falls'
(10 plants from 4" pots)
Plant Profile: Page 150

Iresine 'Blazin Saddle'
or Bloodleaf
(10 plants from 4" pots)
Plant Profile: Page 166

Calibrachoa 'Cabaret Lavender'
(10 plants from 4" pots)
Plant Profile: Page 168

Cultural Information

Light: Light shade to full sun is ideal

Season: Spring through fall for most warmer areas. This plant mix takes temperatures from about 45 degrees to the low 90's.

Lifespan: About three months in this container

Care: Fertilize on planting day with the slow-release mix I describe on page 46. Repeat if the leaves look yellowish or washed out. Pinch back the iresine if it looks leggy.

Water: Water when the plants show signs of wilt or the soil feels dry when you push your fingertip up to your second knuckle into the potting mix. I watered this one every day in mid summer (after it was about a month old) and every other day in cooler weather.

Troubleshooting: No problems

Planting Plan: Easy. Alternate the calibrachoa, iresine, and dicondra in both side layers. Plant the Persian shield in the center. Alternate the smaller plants around the edge, identical to the side layers. *(For full planting demo, see pages 42-43.)*

Container: Kinsman's #ZGBD16 double basket (16"W x 11"D). Go to www.sideplanting.com to find a list of garden center sources near you. To purchase by phone, call 1-800-733-4146 for retail orders or 1-800-733-5613 for wholesale orders. To purchase online: www.kinsmangarden.com for retail and www.kinsmanwholesale.com for wholesale.

Installing the Column: The 42" column is sold in a kit that installs easily and fits this planter well. The product number is ZGBC42. Shop for it at Kinsman Company (contact info under "Container," above). To see a 3.5 minute video of its installation, go to www.sideplanting.com and watch Part 6, *Patio Stands and Border Columns.*

For 3-minute planting video, go to www.sideplanting.com

2ND

16" single basket and stand kit

This arrangement rates a red ribbon (defined on pages 18-19) instead of a blue because it requires one additional chore other than watering: monthly trimming, which only takes about five minutes! However, this plant mix lasts at least the five-to-six month red ribbon minimum in this large container, and the arrangement was trouble free. To get this high performance, be sure to follow the easy planting instructions on pages 42-43.

This basket and stand come in a kit that is quite easy to use.

Dragon Wing Begonia
(1 plant from a three-gallon pot)
Plant Profile: Page 145

Coleus
(8 plants from 4.5" pots)
Plant Profile: Page 148

Creeping Jenny
(8 plants from 4.5" pots)
Plant Profile: Page 149

Wax Begonia
(8 plants from 4.5" pots)
Plant Profile: Page 145

Cultural Information

Light: Light shade to full sun is ideal

Season: Spring through fall for most warmer areas. This plant mix takes temperatures from about 45 degrees to the low 90's.

Lifespan: About six months in this container

Care: Fertilize on planting day with the slow-release mix I describe on page 46. Repeat if the leaves look yellowish or washed out. Pinch back the coleus monthly.

Water: Water when the plants show signs of wilt or the soil feels dry when you push your fingertip up to your second knuckle into the potting mix. I watered this one every day in mid summer (after it was about a month old) and every other day in cooler weather.

Troubleshooting: No problems

Planting Plan: Easy. Alternate the coleus, wax begonia, and creeping Jenny in the side layer. Plant the dragon wing begonia in the center. Alternate the smaller plants around the edge, identical to the side layer. *(For full planting demo, see pages 42-43.)*

Container: This container and stand comes in one kit, Kinsman's Side-Planted Basket Kit, #ZCK16 (basket:16"W x 11"D; base: 14"W; overall height: 35"). Go to www.sideplanting.com to find a list of garden center sources near you. To purchase by phone, call 1-800-733-4146 for retail orders or 1-800-733-5613 for wholesale orders. To purchase online: www.kinsmangarden.com for retail and www.kinsmanwholesale.com for wholesale.

Planting and Putting the Stand Together: I planted this container in the 3-minute *Planting* video at www.sideplanting.com. See the same Web site and watch *Patio Stands and Border Columns* to see the stand being put together, which takes about 30 seconds.

Photo (right) from the home of Joan and Buzz Ahrens in Canton, Georgia.

Spectacular Color

16" single basket and stand kit

This arrangement misses a ribbon because the marigolds and celosia only bloomed for three months. The rest of the plants did quite well for the six-month blue ribbon requirement.

The center container features a basket on a patio stand (see one on the previous page) with the base buried in a large, blue container. After burying it about six inches down, I planted the small plants in the blue container. Be sure your large container is at least 14" wide (on the inside, six inches down) to accommodate the base of the stand.

Serena Angelonia
(3 plants from 4" pots)
Plant Profile: Page 144

Marigolds
(6 plants from 4" pots)
Plant Profile: Page 157

Wax Begonia
(10 plants from 4" pots)
Plant Profile: Page 145

Creeping Jenny
(10 plants from 4" pots)
Plant Profile: Page 149

Celosia
(16 plants from 4" pots)
Plant Profile: Page 166

Cultural Information

Light: Light shade to full sun

Season: Anytime temperatures are between 45 degrees and the low 100's.

Lifespan: The marigolds and celosia only lived about three months. The other plants will live six months in containers this size.

Care: Fertilize on planting day with the slow-release mix I describe on page 46. Repeat if the leaves look yellowish or washed out. Trim the dead flowers off the marigolds, and keep the creeping Jenny in the top basket from growing into the blue container.

Water: Water when the plants show signs of wilt or the soil feels dry when you push your fingertip up to your second knuckle into the potting mix. I watered this one every day in mid summer (after it was about a month old) and every other day in cooler weather.

Troubleshooting: No problems

Planting Plan: Fill the bottom pot with potting mix, to six inches below the rim. Place the stand (shown on page 129) in the pot and bury the base in potting mix, up to about one inch below the rim. Attach the basket on top and plant the side layer with alternated begonias and creeping Jenny. Plant the angelonia along the back, centered, with the marigolds in the center. Tuck in some begonias and creeping Jenny along the front edge. Plant the flowers in the blue pots as shown.

Container: This basket and stand comes in one kit, Kinsman's Side-Planted Basket Kit, #ZCK16 (basket: 16"W x 11"D; base: 14"W; overall height: 35"). Go to www.sideplanting.com to find a list of garden center sources near you. To purchase by phone, call 1-800-733-4146 for retail orders or 1-800-733-5613 for wholesale orders. To purchase online: www.kinsmangarden.com for retail and www.kinsmanwholesale.com for wholesale.

Planting and Putting the Stand Together: I planted a container like this one in the 3-minute *Planting* video at www.sideplanting.com. See the same Web site and watch *Patio Stands an Border Columns* to see the stand put together, which takes about 30 seconds.

For 3-minute planting video, go to www.sideplanting.com

Restful Color

16" single basket and stand kit

This gorgeous arrangement lasted an entire six month growing season. It misses a ribbon, however, because the sweet potato vine grows like Jack-and-the-Bean stalk and attracts bugs.

The center container features a basket on a patio stand (see one on page 129) with the base buried in a large, green container. After burying it about six inches down, I planted the small plants in the green container. Be sure your large container is at least 14" wide (on the inside, six inches down) to accommodate the base of the stand.

Perilla
(1 plant from a one-gallon pot)
Plant Profile: Page 159

Wax Begonia
(16 plants from 4" pots)
Plant Profile: Page 145

Sweet Potato
(8 plants from 4" pots)
Plant Profile: Page 163

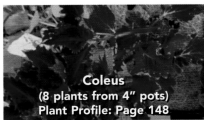
Coleus
(8 plants from 4" pots)
Plant Profile: Page 148

New Guinea Impatiens Sunpatiens
(1 plant from one-gallon pot)
Plant Profile: Page 154

Cultural Information

Light: Light shade to full sun

Season: Anytime temperatures are between 45 degrees and the low 100's. Does better in light shade in temperatures over 93 degrees.

Lifespan: About six months

Care: Fertilize on planting day with the slow-release mix I describe on page 46. Repeat if the leaves look yellowish or washed out. Trim the sweet potato vine monthly to keep it from taking over.

Water: Water when the plants show signs of wilt or the soil feels dry when you push your fingertip up to your second knuckle into the potting mix. I watered this one every day in mid summer (after it was about a month old) and every other day in cooler weather.

Troubleshooting: No problems

Planting Plan: Fill up the bottom pot with potting mix to six inches below the rim. Place the stand (shown on page 129) in the pot, and bury the base in potting mix, up to about one inch below the rim. Attach the basket on top, and plant the side layer with alternated begonias, sweet potato, and coleus. Plant the perilla in the center of the basket. Surround it by alternated begonias, sweet potatoes, and coleus. Plant the flowers in the green pots as shown.

Container: This basket and stand comes in one kit, Kinsman's Side-Planted Basket Kit, #ZCK16 (basket: 16"W x 11"D; base: 14"W; overall height: 35"). Go to www.sideplanting.com to find a list of garden center sources near you. To purchase by phone, call 1-800-733-4146 for retail orders or 1-800-733-5613 for wholesale orders. To purchase online: www.kinsmangarden.com for retail and www.kinsmanwholesale.com for wholesale.

Putting the Stand Together: It takes about 30 seconds to put this stand together. See a short video at www.sideplanting.com called *Patio Stands and Border Columns.*

For 3-minute planting video, go to www.sideplanting.com

Chapter 7

Succulents in Containers:
The Easiest Plants in this Book!

Succulents are the stars of easy container gardening. Since succulents store water in their stems, roots, and leaves, they can go much longer between watering than most other plants. They can also stay in the same pot for years, saving you a lot of repotting work. Here are some more useful information:

❀ Cacti are succulents but somewhat difficult to work with because they don't like regular potting mix, and they have painful spines.

❀ Most other succulents adapt to regular potting mix. Avoid the mixes that include moisture-retaining substances.

❀ Most succulents only need water about once every ten days to three weeks. Since it rains that often in most of the country, you might never have to do anything to them after planting.

❀ Most succulents are cold sensitive, with a few exceptions (like sempervivens). Move them indoors if the temperatures fall to 32 degrees.

❀ Don't use saucers underneath succulents, or they can get too wet.

❀ Handle them gently because most are somewhat fragile.

❀ Some succulents like full sun, while others tolerate shade well.

Above and left: Succulents at the home of Thomas Hobbs, a succulent expert. His fabulous book, "The Jewel Box Garden," gives lots of valuable information about growing these plants.

Easiest Plants Ever!

1ST

This container combo is the easiest I have ever planted. It lasted for a full 18 months (protected from frost) with no watering other than rainfall. That's right - I planted it and never touched it again for its entire lifespan. If you kill this one, please let me know because that would be one for the record books!

The gorgeous, blue strawberry pot is planted with succulents, which are commonly available now in most garden centers. Their durability, coupled with their unique appearance, have made them the rage with container designers.

Agave univitata
(One plant from a 6" pot)
Plant Profile: Page 144

Echeveria spp.
(4 plants from 4" pots)
Plant Profile: Page 151

'String of Bananas'
(3 plants from 3" pots)
Plant Profile: Page 169

Aloe 'Black Doran'
(1 plant from a 4" pot)
Plant Profile: Page 144

Aloe spinossissima
(1 plant from a 4" pot)
Plant Profile: Page 144

Cultural Information

Light: Full sun to light shade

Season: Most succulents take temperatures from 35 to well over 100 degrees.

Lifespan: This arrangement lasted 18 months in this container. It was protected from frost.

Care: Fertilize on planting day with the slow-release mix I describe on page 46. Repeat if the leaves look yellowish or washed-out. That's it! This is a really easy design.

Water: I never watered this container, but it rained at least once a week during its lifespan. Succulents need water every ten days to three weeks. Be sure the potting mix is bone dry before watering. Signs of overwatering include leaf loss and spots of rot. A sign that they need water is shriveled leaves. They need less water in cooler weather than in hotter weather.

Troubleshooting: Watch out for thorns! Otherwise, succulents grow slowly and have few problems with disease or insects. Many of these plants can be maintained in the same pot for a very long time.

Planting Plan: Handle the plants gently; they are fragile. Wear gloves to protect your hands from spines. Plant one large succulent in the top and one or two small ones in each side pocket. Avoid potting mixes that include water-retaining substances.

Container: Anamese blue strawberry jar (24"H x 20"W). The size of the side pockets are a nice feature of this container. They are large enough to fit plants in 4" pots. Most garden centers carry a large variety of succulents in 4" pots, which makes them an ideal choice for the side pockets in this strawberry pot. Go to www.anamese.com for sources.

This container was designed and planted by Alan Stopek of Efflorescence, a nursery in Loxahatchee, Florida (www.efflor.com).

Easiest Plants Ever!

1ST

This container wins a blue ribbon (defined on pages 14-17) because it needed absolutely no care at all except occasional water - and it easily lasted a full six months in this small pot. Succulents are one of the few types of plants that live this long in containers this small.

This is another one of Thomas Hobb's masterpieces. See more information about him on page 135. He not only uses plants but also shells to get this fabulous, textured look.

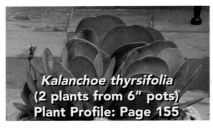

Kalanchoe thyrsifolia
(2 plants from 6" pots)
Plant Profile: Page 155

Agave spp.
(1 plant from 6" pot)
Plant Profile: Page 144

Shell on left
Sempervivens spp. in center
(5 plants from 4" pots)
Plant Profile: Page 162

Echeveria spp.
(6 plants from 4" pots)
Plant Profile: Page 151

Burro's Tail
(2 plants from 4" pots)
Plant Profile: Page 146

Cultural Information

Light: Full sun to light shade

Season: Most succulents take temperatures from 35 to well over 100 degrees.

Lifespan: These plants last about 18 months in a container this size if protected from frost.

Care: Fertilize on planting day with the slow-release mix I describe on page 46. Repeat if the leaves look yellowish or washed out. That's it! This is a really easy design.

Water: Succulents need water every ten days to three weeks. Be sure the potting mix is bone dry before watering. Signs of over-watering include leaf loss and spots of rot. A sign that they need water is shriveled leaves. They need less water in cooler weather than in hotter weather.

Troubleshooting: No problems! Succulents grow slowly and have few problems with disease or insects.

Planting Plan: Handle the plants gently; they are fragile. Wear gloves to protect your hands from spines. Duplicate these containers by following the design in the photos. Plant succulents very close together.

Most garden centers now have many different succulents. Choose the ones you like. Vary the leaf sizes (try the succulent with the largest leaf next to the one with the smallest) as well as the colors.

Container: Low terra cotta saucers mixed with terra cotta bowls

Easiest Plants Ever!

1ST

This arrangement rates a blue ribbon (defined on pages 14-17) because it needed absolutely no care at all except water - and it lasted a full, six months in this pot. To get this high performance, be sure to follow the easy planting instructions on pages 44-45.

Succulents are combined with dicondra 'Silver Falls', which also likes it on the dry side.

This is another one of Thomas Hobbs' masterpieces. See more information about him on page 135.

Echeveria spp.
(3 plants from 4" pots)
Plant Profile: Page 151

Sempervivens spp.
(2 plants from 4" pots)
Plant Profile: Page 162

Echeveria spp.
(3 plants from 4" pots)
Plant Profile: Page 151

Sempervivens spp.
(2 plants from 4" pots)
Plant Profile: Page 162

Dicondra 'Silver Falls'
(3 plants from 4" pots)
Plant Profile: Page 150

Cultural Information

Light: Full sun to light shade

Season: Most succulents take temperatures from 35 to well over 100 degrees.

Lifespan: These plants last about 18 months in a container this size if protected from frost.

Care: Fertilize on planting day with the slow-release mix I describe on page 46. Repeat if the leaves look yellowish or washed out. That's it! This is a really easy design.

Water: Succulents need water every ten days to three weeks. Be sure the potting mix is bone dry before watering. Signs of over-watering include leaf loss and spots of rot. A sign that they need water is shriveled leaves. They need less water in cooler weather than in hotter weather.

Troubleshooting: No problems! Succulents grow slowly and have few problems with disease or insects.

Planting Plan: Handle the plants gently; they are fragile.

Duplicate these containers by following the design in the photos. Plant succulents very close together.

Most garden centers now have many different succulents. Choose the ones you like. Vary the leaf sizes (try the succulent with the largest leaf next to the one with the smallest) as well as the colors. Succulents combine with other plants as well. The long, silver vine is dicondra 'Silver Falls,' which is not a succulent.

Container: Cast stone urn

Chapter 8

Best Container Plants

This chapter includes the results of many years of plant trials. It takes the guess work out of choosing many plants from your garden centers, describing both the good and the bad about them. Take it with you so you can check them out before you buy.

Above: Tall snapdragons form the centerpiece of this white bowl. They look great when all the flowers bloom at once. One caution: The snapdragons all stop blooming at the same time while new buds are forming. The flowers re-appear in about a month later. Other flowers included in the arrangement include dark purple violas, marigolds, and lavender lantana.

The bowl was planted with large plants shortly before this photo was taken. The plants were so large compared with the size of the pot that the arrangement only lasted about six weeks. But the low cost, coupled with the ease of planting, made it well worth the time and money.

Left: This window box arrangement is the most beautiful one I have ever planted. But, I was disappointed when it only lasted three months instead of the six month period I was hoping for. I don't know if the short lifespan had anything to do with the high, 95 degree plus temperatures that began at the same time this arrangement faded.

Plants include orange geraniums, yellow calibrachoa, 'Suncatcher Hot Pink' petunias and Supertunia 'Royal Velvet' petunias.

The container is Kinsman's #CLZW36 window box (36"L x 9"W x 9"D). For sources, see page 114 under "Container."

Plant Profiles: The High Performers

Agave (*Agave spp.*)

1ST

Agaves not only offer bold, tropical texture but are also very easy to grow, particularly since they don't need much water. Look for one of the 300 different varieties with no spines.

Care: Very easy. Plant with slow-release fertilizer described on page 46, and leave them alone! Fertilize again in 6 to 9 months. Carefully remove the old leaves when they die.

Water: Low. Every 10 to 20 days.

Season: All year. Protect from frost unless you are using one that is hardy.

Light: Light shade to full sun

Zone: Most grow in zones 10-11 but some grow as far north as zone 6.

Pest problems: Occasional snails

Use: Centerpiece or single specimen

Size: Many different sizes available, up to 6 feet tall by 6 feet wide.

Colors: Green, silvery green, or variegated.

Average life: 10 to 30 years

Cautions: Many (but not all) agaves have very sharp tips that can inflict significant injury. And, the sap is a serious skin toxin, so be sure to wear long sleeves and gloves when trimming. Do not touch your eyes with the sap, or you could get a nasty infection.

Aloe (*Aloe spp.*)

1ST

Aloes are succulents that are really easy to grow. Some, like *Aloe vera*, have a medicinal sap that is good for many ailments. There are over 300 kinds of aloe.

Care: Very easy. Plant with slow-release fertilizer described on page 46, and leave them alone! Fertilize again in 6 to 9 months. Carefully remove the old leaves when they die.

Water: Low. Every 10 to 20 days. Often lives on rainwater alone.

Season: All year. Bring inside if frost threatens.

Light: Light shade to full sun

Zone: 10 to 11. Protect from freezes.

Pest problems: None serious

Use: Centerpiece or accent

Size: Varies greatly by species, from tiny to over 30 feet tall.

Colors: Gray to green

Average life: 10 to 30 years

Cautions: Serrated leaves on some varieties can be quite hazardous.

Angelonia (*Angelonia spp.*)

Angelonia has been an erratic performer in my trials. Look for 'Serena' angelonia, which never stopped blooming for six months. When it works, angelonia is a gorgeous plant.

Care: Plant with slow-release fertilizer described on page 46, and leave them alone!

Water: Medium. Up to every day in hot summers.

Season: When temperatures range from 45 to 100 degrees.

Light: Full sun to light shade

Zone: Protect from freezes.

Pest problems: None known

Use: Centerpiece or accent

Size: Varies from 8 to 18 inches long

Colors: White, pink, and different shade of lavender.

Average life: The 'Serena' series lasts about 6 months. Some of the others I tried lasted only a month or so.

Cautions: None known

 Blue ribbon plants defined on pages 14-15.

Anthurium *(Anthurium spp.)*

1ST

Anthuriums bloom all the time, need very little care or water, and can stay in the same pot for at least a year. They also bloom in less light than any other plant in this book.

Care: Very easy. Plant with slow-release fertilizer described on page 46, and leave them alone! Fertilize again in 6 to 9 months.

Water: Low. We watered ours once a week. It tolerates quite a bit more water if planted with thirsty plants.

Season: Anthuriums bloom all year. Protect them from temperatures under 45 degrees. I can't keep them in bloom inside the house.

Light: Deep to medium shade. The leaves burn with even a little sun.

Zone: 11 for outside use during the coldest days of winter.

Pest problems: Holes in the leaves usually come from snails; also, leaf spot diseases.

Use: Centerpiece or accent

Size: The different types average 12 to 18 inches tall by 6 to 12 inches wide.

Colors: Pink, peach, orange, red, and white

Average life: 2 to 10 years

Cautions: Irritant

Begonia, Dragon Wing *(Begonia 'Dragon Wing')*

1ST

Dragon wing begonias are one of the highest performers in our trials, blooming continually with an impressive percentage of color for at least six months.

Care: Very easy. Plant with slow-release fertilizer described on page 46, and leave them alone! Fertilize again in 6 to 9 months. Trim off the tips if the plants become too large.

Water: Medium

Season: Any frost-free season

Light: Medium shade to full sun. Needs some break from sun if temperatures stay consistently about 94 degrees.

Zone: Use as an annual. Tolerant of light frost but not a freeze.

Pest problems: Occasional fungus, caterpillars, or snails.

Use: Mounding or centerpiece plant. One of the best plants for the sides of a side-planted container.

Size: In the top of a large container, grows 2 feet tall by 1 foot wide. Smaller if planted in the side of a basket, about 8 inches tall.

Colors: Red or pink

Average life: 6 to 12 months if protected from frost.

Cautions: None known

Begonia, Wax *(Begonia x semper. Cultorum)*

1ST

Wax begonias are one of the highest performers in our trials. They never go out of bloom and live happily for a full, six month period.

Care: Very easy. Plant with slow-release fertilizer described on page 46, and leave them alone!

Water: Low, but tolerates daily watering if planted with impatiens.

Season: Any frost-free season. Prefers temperatures below the high-90's.

Light: Medium shade to full sun in the cooler areas, but some burn in the summer sun. Bronze-leafed varieties, as well as new, sun-tolerant green ones, are more sun-tolerant in the heat.

Zone: Use as an annual. Tolerant of light frost but not a freeze.

Pest problems: Occasional fungus, shown by leaf spots.

Use: Mounding plant

Size: In the top of a container, grows about 8 inches tall by 5 inches wide. Smaller if planted in the side of a basket, about 4 to 6 inches tall.

Colors: Red, pink, or white flowers on green or bronze leaves.

Average life: 5 to 6 months

Cautions: None known

Plant Profiles: The High Performers

Bromeliad *(many different genuses and species)*

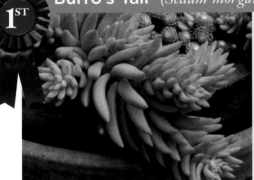

Bromeliads are one of the highest performers in our trials. Some have gorgeous flowers that bloom for two to four months at a time. They are quite happy in the same pot for years on end.

Care: See directions on page 46. Avoid getting fertilizer in the center of the plants. The mother plant dies after flowering and producing pups (babies). See page 54 to learn how to separate them.

Water: Low, but tolerates daily watering if planted with impatiens.

Season: All year. Bring inside if frost threatens.

Light: Medium to light shade. Takes more light in winter. If used inside, will continue to bloom in deep shade until that flower dies. Some thick-leafed varieties take full sun.

Zone: 9b to 11. Protect from freezes.

Pest problems: None serious

Use: Centerpiece or accent

Size: Varies greatly by species, from tiny to over 5 feet tall.

Colors: All!

Average life: Single plant lives about 2 years but sends up babies to replace itself.

Cautions: Serrated leaves on some varieties can be quite hazardous.

Burro's Tail *(Sedum morganianum)*

Burro's tail is a succulent that is really easy to grow. It is ideal for hanging baskets because of its ability to trail over the sides.

Care: Very easy. Plant with slow-release fertilizer described on page 46, and leave them alone! Fertilize again in 6 to 9 months.

Water: Medium

Season: Plant when temperatures vary between 45 degrees and the low-100's.

Light: Light shade to full sun

Zone: Protect from frost.

Pest problems: None known

Use: Trailing plant

Size: Trails as long as 8 feet down the side of a container.

Colors: Greyish green

Average life: 2 to 10 years

Cautions: Unknown

Cabbage or Kale, Ornamental *(Brassica oleracea)*

Ornamental Cabbage was an outstanding performer in our container trials. This cool weather plant thrived in temperatures from the low-20's to the mid-70's.

Care: Very easy. Plant with slow-release fertilizer described on page 46, and leave them alone! Fertilize again in 6 to 9 months.

Water: Medium

Season: Plant when temperatures vary between 25 degrees and the mid-70's.

Light: Light shade to full sun

Zone: Use as an annual.

Pest problems: None known

Use: Side or edge plant. Did quite well in the sides of side-planted containers. Too short to be a good centerpiece.

Size: The different types average 12 to 18 inches tall by 6 to 12 inches wide.

Colors: Pink, peach, orange, red, and white.

Average life: 6 months

Cautions: Unknown

Blue ribbon plants are defined on pages 14-15.

Cactus *(Cactus spp.)*

Cacti are succulents but need special, cactus soil instead of regular potting mix. Watch out for dangerous spines. Cacti are easy if you don't overwater them.

Care: Very easy. Plant in a free-draining cactus mix with slow-release fertilizer described on page 46, and leave them alone! Fertilize again in 6 to 9 months.

Water: Low. Be sure the potting mix is quite dry before watering.

Season: Depends on variety. Some are tropical and some tolerate freezes.

Light: Different varieties tolerate different amounts of light - from medium shade to full sun.

Zone: Depends on variety

Pest problems: Mealybugs, fungus

Use: Centerpiece or accent

Size: Range from tiny to over 30 feet tall.

Colors: Green with many different flower colors.

Average life: 2 to 10 years in containers.

Cautions: Spines

Caladium *(Caladium x hortulanum)*

Caladiums are one of the highest performers for summer color. I used them extensively as centerpieces. Be sure you know the mature size of the ones you buy.

Care: Very easy. For instant effects, plant full-size plants rather than tubers. Plant with slow-release fertilizer described on page 46, and leave them alone!

Water: Medium

Season: Summer. Does best in temperatures of over 62 degrees.

Light: Medium shade to full sun. Needs some break from sun if temperatures stay consistently about 94 degrees.

Zone: Grown throughout the world as a summer annual.

Pest problems: Slugs or snails

Use: Mounding plant or centerpiece

Size: 6 to 30 inches tall, depending on variety.

Colors: Shades of white, green, red, and pink.

Average life: 6 months

Cautions: Poisonous

Canna Lily *(Canna x generalis)*

Cannas rate a red ribbon instead of a blue ribbon because they have a tendency to get pests. Other than that, they are terrific centerpiece plants for summer containers.

Care: Very easy. Plant with slow-release fertilizer described on page 46, and leave them alone! Trim off dead flowers if you have time.

Water: Medium

Season: Cannas are perennials that are most often used as summer annuals.

Light: Full sun

Zone: 7 to 10

Pest problems: Fungus and caterpillars

Use: Mounding plant

Size: 3 to 5 feet tall by 2 to 3 feet wide. Dwarfs grow about 2 feet tall in a container.

Colors: Pink, yellow, peach, coral, red, and orange flowers. Leaves come in bronze, green, purple, or burgundy, solid or striped.

Average life: They average about one summer in the same container, but I had some that lasted for up to 2 years in frost-free locations.

Cautions: None known

Red ribbon plants are defined on pages 18-19.

Plant Profiles: The High Performers

Chenille Plant *(Acalypha hispida)*

Chenille plants are not well known outside of the subtropics. They make excellent summer container plants in most of the country.

Care: Very easy. Plant with slow-release fertilizer described on page 46, and leave them alone! Fertilize again in 6 to 9 months.

Water: Medium

Season: Use when temperatures range from 40 to over 100 degrees.

Light: Full sun to light shade

Zone: 10b to 11 for outside. In cooler zones, move containers inside if cold threatens.

Pest problems: None known

Use: Centerpiece or accent

Size: From 3 to 8 feet tall

Colors: Green leaves with long, red, fuzzy flowers.

Average life: 15 to 20 years in frost-free locations. Plant in your garden (in frost-free areas) when it outgrows your container.

Cautions: None known

Chenille Plant, Dwarf *(Acalypha pendula)*

Dwarf chenille is an easy and attractive plant for the edges of pots and baskets. Since it grows in sun or shade, it works well in most summer environments.

Care: Very easy. Plant with slow-release fertilizer described on page 46 and fertilize again in 6 to 9 months. Trim off the tips if the plants become too large.

Water: Medium

Season: Plant when temperatures vary between 45 degrees and the low-100's.

Light: Medium shade to full sun

Zone: 7 to 11. Dies back in a freeze but grows back when the weather warms up.

Pest problems: None known

Use: Trailing plant

Size: About 3 to 4 inches tall by 6 to 10 inches wide. This plant is a short trailer, growing about 6 to 8 inches down the sides of the pot.

Colors: Red

Average life: 2 to 10 years

Cautions: Unknown

Coleus *(Solenostemon scutellarioides)*

Coleus are one of the highest performers in our trials, thriving as centerpieces or planted in the sides. They just miss a blue ribbon because they require monthly trimming.

Care: Very easy. Plant with slow-release fertilizer described on page 46. Pinch the tips monthly if plant becomes too large. If you delay this trimming, it may take them a while to look good again.

Water: Medium

Season: Whenever temperatures are above 38 degrees.

Light: Light shade to full sun

Zone: Use as an annual.

Pest problems: Occasional aphids, mites, mealybugs, slugs, and snails.

Use: Smaller types for mounding plants and larger ones for centerpieces. Does quite well planted through the side holes of a side-planted container.

Size: Varies greatly by variety, 6 to 36 inches tall and equally as wide.

Colors: Shades of red, white, yellow, and green and purple.

Average life: 6 months

Cautions: Unknown

Blue ribbon plants are defined on pages 14-15.

Copper Leaf 'Ceylon' *(Acalypha 'Ceylon')*

Copperleafs are good centerpiece plants for containers, especially in the summer. They take heat very well and rate a blue ribbon.

Care: Very easy. Plant with slow-release fertilizer described on page 46, and leave them alone! Fertilize again in 6 to 9 months. Trim off the tips if they become quite long.

Water: Medium

Season: Use when temperatures range from 40 to over 100 degrees.

Light: Full sun to light shade

Zone: 10b to 11 for outside. In cooler zones, move containers inside if cold threatens.

Pest problems: None known

Use: Centerpiece or accent

Size: From 3 to 8 feet tall

Colors: Rust leaves

Average life: 15 to 20 years in frost-free locations. Plant in your garden (in frost-free areas) when it outgrows your container.

Cautions: None known

Creeping Jenny *(Lysimachia mummularia)*

Creeping Jenny is one of the best trailing plants for containers. It is easy to grow - and quick to reach a good size without overwhelming the other plants.

Care: Very easy. Plant with slow-release fertilizer described on page 46 and fertilize again in 6 to 9 months. Trim off the tips if the plants become too large.

Water: Medium

Season: All year in frost free areas. Dies back in a frost but returns in zones 3 to 11.

Light: Medium shade to full sun

Zone: 3-9 as a perennial. Use as an annual in zones 10-11.

Pest problems: None known

Use: Trailing plant. Does quite well planted through the side holes of a side-planted container.

Size: Trails over the edge of the pot to at least 18 inches, but it takes a while to get there!

Colors: Lime green

Average life: Long term perennial in zones 3-9.

Cautions: Unknown

Croton *(Codiaeum variegatum)*

Crotons are one of the easiest plants for containers. They are happy in the same pot for years on end and require little care. There are hundreds of different varieties, all of which take heat well.

Care: Very easy. Plant with slow-release fertilizer described on page 46, and leave them alone! Fertilize again in 6 to 9 months.

Water: Medium

Season: Use when temperatures range from 40 to over 100 degrees.

Light: Medium shade to full sun

Zone: 10a to 11 for outside. In cooler zones, move containers inside if cold threatens.

Pest problems: Occasional scale, mealybugs, and spider mites.

Use: Centerpiece or mounding plant

Size: Varies greatly by variety, from dwarfs to small trees.

Colors: Shades of red, yellow, green, pink, grey, black, and orange.

Average life: 15 to 20 years. Plant in your garden (in frost-free areas) when it outgrows your container. Lasts about 1 year in the same pot.

Cautions: Milky sap irritates skin and stains clothes.

Red ribbon plants are defined on pages 18-19.

Plant Profiles: The High Performers

Daisy, California Bush *(Gamolepis chrysanthemoides)*

California bush daisy (yellow flower, above) is one of the highest performing daisies from our trials. It blooms almost continuously for at least six months.

Care: Very easy. Plant with slow-release fertilizer described on page 46, and leave them alone! Fertilize again in 6 to 9 months.

Water: Medium

Season: Prefers temperatures between 35 and 90 degrees.

Light: Light shade to full sun

Zone: Although this plant is used as a perennial in other warm parts of the world, it performs best as an annual in most areas. Protect from frost.

Pest problems: Spider mites occasionally. I have never had a pest on this plant in my gardens.

Use: Centerpiece or accent

Size: About 18 inches tall by 12 inches wide

Colors: Yellow

Average life: Looks good for about 6 months in the same container.

Cautions: Unknown

Dicondra 'Silver Falls' *(Dicondra 'Silver Falls')*

Dicondra 'Silver Falls' is a fabulous, silver vine that is one of the best container plants. It requires almost no care and gives incredible performance.

Care: Very easy. Plant with slow-release fertilizer described on page 46, and leave them alone! Trim if it hits the ground.

Water: Low. Do not overwater.

Season: Plant when temperatures vary between 45 degrees and the low-100's. This plant is not cold tolerant at all.

Light: Light shade to full sun

Zone: Use as an annual.

Pest problems: None known

Use: Trailing plant. Does quite well planted through the side holes of a side-planted container.

Size: Trails down as far as 8 feet

Colors: Silver

Average life: Six months

Cautions: Unknown

Dieffenbachia *(Dieffenbachia spp.)*

Dieffenbachia is one of the easiest house plants around. It also does well outside, although the leaves burn when the temperatures dip below 45 degrees. It grows well in dense shade, one of the few that will.

Care: Very easy. Plant with slow-release fertilizer described on page 46, and leave them alone! Fertilize again in 6 to 9 months. Trim off brown leaves. Trim back branches if plant becomes leggy.

Water: Medium

Season: All year, but protect from temperatures as low as the mid-40's.

Light: Medium to dense shade

Zone: Used throughout the world as a houseplant. Outdoors, zone 11 is the safest. I used it outdoors in zone 10a for several years with no problems, but a cold spell finally damaged them.

Pest problems: Mites, mealybugs, and aphids.

Use: Centerpiece or accent

Size: Most varieties average about 2 feet tall in a container.

Colors: Leaves are variegated in shades of bright green, lime green, and white.

Average life: Lives many years in containers if root-pruned annually.

Cautions: Highly toxic. Sap is a skin irritant. Poisonous if eaten.

 Blue ribbon plants are defined on pages 14-15.

Diplademia *(Mandevillea spp.)*

Diplademia blooms in summer, even in high temperatures. Treat it like an annual and it will require nothing but water!

Care: Very easy. Plant with slow-release fertilizer described on page 46, and leave them alone!

Water: Medium

Season: Plant when temperatures vary between 65 degrees and the low-100's.

Light: Light shade to full sun

Zone: Use as an annual.

Pest problems: None known

Use: Centerpiece or accent

Size: The different types average 12 to 18 inches tall by equally as wide.

Colors: Pink

Average life: 6 months

Cautions: Unknown

Dracaena *(Dracaena spp.)*

Dracaenas are one of the most common indoor plants. They work well outdoors as well, provided they are protected from frost. And just add water! They are really easy.

Care: Very easy. Plant with slow-release fertilizer described on page 46, and leave them alone! Fertilize again in 6 to 9 months.

Water: Low, but adapt to high water if combined with flowers that require it.

Season: All year. Protect from frost.

Light: Dense to light shade

Zone: 10 to 11. Protect from freezes in cooler area if used outdoors.

Pest problems: Scales and mealybugs, particularly if used indoors or under screening. I've never seen a pest on this plant outdoors.

Use: Centerpiece or accent

Size: Vary from 1 to 30 feet tall

Colors: Depends on variety. There are many different kinds of dracaenas.

Average life: 10 to 15 years if moved inside when freezes threaten.

Cautions: Unknown

Echeveria *(Echeveria spp.)*

Echeverias are one of the easiest plants to grow because they require so little water. They are succulents and their leaves resemble rosettes. Many different types are available.

Care: Very easy. Plant with slow-release fertilizer described on page 46, and leave them alone! Fertilize again in 6 to 9 months.

Water: Low, particularly in cool weather. They don't like wet leaves when it is cold.

Season: Protect from frost.

Light: Light shade to full sun; leaves have better color in part sun, part shade.

Zone: 10-11. Used as a summer annual in areas that are colder.

Pest problems: None known

Use: Edge plant

Size: From 6 to 18 inches wide

Colors: Green, white, blue, pink, gray, orange, red, or brown.

Average life: 2 to 10 years

Cautions: Take care because they are fragile to handle.

Red ribbon plants are defined on pages 18-19.

Plant Profiles: The High Performers

Elephant Ear *(Alocasia or Colocasia spp.)*

Elephant ears are fabulous centerpiece plants that require very little care. Just plant a large one surrounded by small trailers and you have instant, easy impact.

Care: Very easy. Plant with slow-release fertilizer described on page 46, and leave them alone! Trim off the dead leaves.

Water: Medium

Season: Plant when temperatures vary between 45 degrees and the low-100's.

Light: Medium shade to full sun

Zone: 8 to 11

Pest problems: None known

Use: Centerpiece or accent

Size: Size varies by type, from 1 to 8 feet tall.

Colors: Various shades of green and black.

Average life: Depends on the cultivar

Cautions: Sap can irritate skin. Don't let children eat this one.

Geranium *(Pelargonium x hortorum)*

Geraniums rate a red ribbon because they look better with the dead flowers removed. They thrive in containers and are one of our best choices for centerpieces.

Care: Plant with slow-release fertilizer described on page 46. Geraniums look better with the dead flowers removed, which can be tedious. I sometimes let them go and am surprised at how well they do!

Water: Medium to low

Season: Prefers temperatures between 35 and 90 degrees.

Light: Light shade to full sun

Zone: Although this plant is used as a perennial in other warm parts of the world, it performs best as an annual in most areas. Protect from frost.

Pest problems: Spider mites occasionally. I have never had a pest on this plant in my gardens.

Use: Centerpiece or accent

Size: 12 to 14 inches tall

Colors: Many shades of red, pink, peach, white, and lavender.

Average life: 5 to 6 months

Cautions: Unknown

Grass, Dwarf White Striped Sweet Flag *(Acorus gramineus)*

This grass did beautifully in our trials. Small, white grasses are both useful and unusual. This one breezes through an entire growing season with no problems.

Care: Very easy. Plant with slow-release fertilizer described on page 46, and leave them alone!

Water: Medium, but also tolerates wet conditions.

Season: Plant when temperatures vary between 45 degrees and the low-100's.

Light: Light shade

Zone: 5-11

Pest problems: None known

Use: Centerpiece or accent

Size: About 12 inches tall

Colors: Green and white striped

Average life: About 6 months in a container.

Cautions: None known

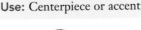 **Blue ribbon plants are defined on pages 14-15.**

Grass, Fiber Optic *(Scirpus cernuus a.k.a Isolepsis cernuus)*

Fiber optic grass features tiny, grass-like leaves with minute yellow spikes on the tips of each leaf, giving the illusion of a fiber optic lamp. And talk about easy!

Care: Very easy. Plant with slow-release fertilizer described on page 46, and leave them alone!

Water: Adapts to somewhat dry or very wet conditions.

Season: Plant when temperatures vary between 45 degrees and the low-100's.

Light: Medium to light shade

Zone: 8 to 11. Tolerant of light frost

Pest problems: None known

Use: Mounding plant that works well in the center or along the edges of any pot.

Size: In my trials, grew to about 6 inches tall by equally as wide.

Colors: Green

Average life: Looked good for about 6 months in a container.

Cautions: Unknown

Grass, Fountain *(Pennisetum spp.)*

Fountain grass has a tall, graceful form. It looks good when not blooming, but better when the fuzzy seed fronds form. They last a month or so. And, fountain grass is easy to care for.

Care: Very easy. Plant with slow-release fertilizer described on page 46, and leave them alone! Fertilize again in 6 to 9 months.

Water: Low

Season: Protect from frost because it dies back in freezing weather.

Light: Light shade to full sun

Zone: Hardy to zone 4

Pest problems: None known in pots

Use: Centerpiece

Size: In the top of a container, grows about 3 feet by 2.5 feet wide.

Colors: Green, bronze, gray

Average life: 6 months

Cautions: Unknown

Grass, Juncus *(Juncus effusus)*

Juncus is one of the best grasses for centerpieces. Its tall stature keeps it well above most plants used for edge plantings. And it is incredibly easy to grow!

Care: Very easy. Plant with slow-release fertilizer described on page 46, and leave them alone! Fertilize again in 6 to 9 months.

Water: Low to high. Very adaptable to what is needed by the plants around it.

Season: Dies back somewhat when the temperatures hit the low 20's. Best used in spring, summer, and fall.

Light: Light shade to full sun

Zone: Hardy to zone 4

Pest problems: None known

Use: Centerpiece or accent

Size: 15 to 24 inches tall

Colors: Green

Average life: Perennial to zone 4. Exact lifespan unknown.

Cautions: Unknown

Red ribbon plants are defined on pages 18-19.

Plant Profiles: The High Performers

Grass, New England Hair Sedge *(Carex comans 'Frosted Curls')*

New Zealand hair sedge offers a unique trailing habit that is quite unusual for grasses, which are normally upright. It is extremely easy to grow and lasts all season.

Care: Very easy. Plant with slow-release fertilizer described on page 46, and leave them alone!

Water: We watered ours every 3 days, but it seems pretty adaptive.

Season: Any frost-free season

Light: Light shade to full sun

Zone: 7 to 11

Pest problems: None known

Use: Slightly trailing

Size: About 12 inches over the edge of the pot at maturity.

Colors: Greyish green

Average life: 6 to 8 months in our container trials.

Cautions: Unknown

Impatiens *(Impatiens wallerana)*

Impatiens are the world's most popular annual plants. They literally bloom their heads off from the day you put them in till the day you take them out.

Care: Very easy. Plant with slow-release fertilizer described on page 46, and leave them alone!

Water: High. Containers with impatiens are great candidates for drip irrigation.

Season: Perform best in temperatures of 40 to 90 degrees, but grow in shade into the high 90's.

Light: Medium shade to full sun. Avoid sun in high temperatures or long, sunny days.

Zone: Use as annual. Very susceptible to frost.

Pest problems: Fungus and slugs

Use: Mounding plant that works well alone or mixed with other bright colors.

Size: Generally, in containers, they get 12 inches tall by equally as wide.

Colors: Red, salmon, orange, white, purple or pink.

Average life: 6 months

Cautions: Very high water use

Impatiens, New Guinea *(Impatiens x New Guinea Hybrids)*

New Guinea impatiens have more color impact than any other plant you can use in a container. Both their flowers and leaves are colorful, with the most color coming from the flowers.

Care: Very easy. Plant with slow-release fertilizer described on page 46, and leave them alone!

Water: High, but not as much as regular impatiens.

Season: Perform best in temperatures of 40 to 90 degrees, but bloom well in shade into the high 90's.

Light: Medium shade to full sun. Avoid sun in high temperatures or long, sunny days.

Zone: Use as an annual. Very sensitive to the slightest frost.

Pest problems: Fungus, slugs, Japanese beetles. These pests cause them to get a red ribbon instead of a blue.

Use: Mounding plant that works well as a centerpiece or in the sides.

Size: About 8 to 12 inches tall in the top of a container, smaller in the sides.

Colors: Iridescent pinks, oranges, reds, purples, peaches, whites, and multi-colored.

Average life: 5 to 6 months

Cautions: Unknown

Blue ribbon plants are defined on pages 14-15.

Impatiens, Double *(Impatiens spp.)*

Double impatiens bloom all season with gorgeous, rose-like blooms. Use them in locations where you can see the flower up close.

Care: Very easy. Plant with slow-release fertilizer described on page 46, and leave them alone!

Water: Medium in shade and very high in sun - as much as twice a day. Good candidate for drip irrigation.

Season: Perform best in temperatures of 40 to 90 degrees, but grow in shade into the high 90's.

Light: Medium shade to full sun. Avoid sun in high temperatures or, long, sunny days.

Zone: Very sensitive to the lightest frost so bring them indoors.

Pest problems: Fungus and slugs

Use: Mounding plant

Size: Grows to 18 inches tall as a centerpiece. Grows about 8 to 12 inches tall in the sides of side-planted containers.

Colors: Red, pink, purple, orange, peach, and white.

Average life: 5 to 6 months

Cautions: Unknown

Ivy *(Hedera helix)*

Ivy is one of the best trailing plants for shade. It requires little water or trimming, making it the ideal blue ribbon plant.

Care: Very easy. Plant with slow-release fertilizer described on page 46, and leave them alone! Fertilize again in 6 to 9 months. Trim if it reaches the ground.

Water: Low, but adapts to higher water if planted with more thirsty plants.

Season: Varies with type. Some grow all year, while others die in very cold weather.

Light: Sun to dense shade in winter. Shade in summer.

Zone: Varies with type

Pest problems: Scale and mold

Use: Trailing plant. Does quite well planted through the side holes of a side-planted container.

Size: Trails about 12 to 36 inches down the sides of the pot during one summer, depending on type.

Colors: Green or variegated

Average life: Lives for many years

Cautions: Unknown

Kalanchoe *(Kalanchoe thyrsifolia)*

This kalanchoe is simple to grow for a full season with nothing but water! It is another succulent star, adding coarse texture to any arrangement.

Care: Very easy. Plant with slow-release fertilizer described on page 46, and leave them alone!

Water: Low

Season: Protect from frost

Light: Light shade to full sun

Zone: 10-11

Pest problems: None known

Use: Centerpiece or accent

Size: Grows quite tall eventually, to about 18 inches.

Colors: Greyish green

Average life: Years in frost free areas

Cautions: Unknown

Red ribbon plants are defined on pages 18-19.

Plant Profiles: The High Performers

Lamium *(Lamium maculatum 'White Nancy')*

Lamium are easy plants that last all season with very little care. They look particularly good mixed with pink and purple flowers.

Care: Very easy. Plant with slow-release fertilizer described on page 46, and leave them alone!

Water: Medium

Season: For containers, spring, summer, and fall. Winter in frost-free areas.

Light: Medium shade to full sun in the cooler weather, but burns in the summer sun.

Zone: Hardy to zone 3

Pest problems: None known

Use: Trailing plant for edges or sides

Size: Trails about 8 inches down the side of a pot.

Colors: Green and white leaves with small, white flowers. Use this plant for its leaves.

Average life: Perennial. Lifespan unknown.

Cautions: Unknown

Lantana *(Lantana spp.)*

Lantana grow well in hot, dry areas. Look for older varieties. Some of the new ones we tried went in and out of bloom. Excellent for hot temperatures and lots of butterflies.

Care: Very easy. Plant with slow-release fertilizer described on page 46, and leave them alone!

Water: Medium in containers. Low in the ground.

Season: Purple peaks in temperatures from 32 to 85 degrees. Other colors peak in temperatures from 70 to the low 100's.

Light: Light shade to full sun

Zone: Use as an annual. Some grow as perennials to zone 8.

Pest problems: Occasional fungus, and whitefly. Do not overwater.

Use: Trailing or mounding varieties

Size: Expect trailers to grow 12 inches down the edge of the pot. The upright variety will grow 2 feet tall in a pot.

Colors: Yellow, purple, red, orange, and white.

Average life: 2 to 4 months in container.

Cautions: Poisonous to humans and pets. Can cause serious illness or death.

Licorice Plant, Silver *(Helichrysum petiolare 'Silver Licorice')*

Silver Licorice is one of the toughest container plants I know. It thrives in cool or hot temperatures, sun or light shade. The color is a lot of fun to work with, particularly with pink and purple.

Care: Very easy. Plant with slow-release fertilizer described on page 46, and leave them alone!

Water: Medium

Season: Plant when temperatures vary between 45 degrees and the low-100's.

Light: Light shade to full sun

Zone: Use as an annual. Tolerant of light frost but not a freeze.

Pest problems: No pest problems in our trials. I have heard of whiteflies and crown and stem rot in cool, damp conditions.

Use: Trailing plant. Does quite well planted through the side holes of a side-planted container.

Size: 8 to 12 inches tall and equally as wide.

Colors: Silvery gray

Average life: 6 months

Cautions: Unknown

Blue ribbon plants are defined on pages 14-15.

Lysimachia 'Outback Sunset' *(Lysimachia 'Outback Sunset')*

Outback Sunset is a great, colorful plant. The bright color of the leaves is quite showy, and this plant is very easy to grow, performing extremely well in our trials. Use it for the leaves rather than the flowers.

Care: Very easy. Plant with slow-release fertilizer described on page 46, and leave them alone!

Water: Medium

Season: Plant when temperatures vary between 45 degrees and the low-100's.

Light: Medium shade to full sun

Zone: Hardy to zone 7a

Pest problems: None known

Use: Trailing plant for sides or edges. Does quite well planted through the side holes of a side-planted container.

Size: Grows about 8 inches down the sides of a pot.

Colors: Yellow and green leaves with yellow flowers.

Average life: 4 to 6 months

Cautions: Unknown

Marigolds *(Tagetes spp.)*

Marigolds were not my favorite yellow plant during our container trials. They didn't last anywhere near as long as other yellows we tried, like melampodium during the warm season, or violas during the cool season.

Care: Plant with slow-release fertilizer described on page 46. Remove the dead flowers.

Water: Medium

Season: Plant when temperatures vary between 32 degrees and the low-90's.

Light: Light shade to full sun

Zone: Use as an annual

Pest problems: Occasional spider mites, particularly in dry weather

Use: Mounding plant or centerpiece

Size: From 6 to 30 inches tall, depending on variety.

Colors: Yellow, orange, burnt orange, white, and burgundy.

Average life: 2 months

Cautions: Unknown

Melampodium *(Melampodium paludosum)*

Melampodium is one of my favorite yellow-flowering container plants. It blooms well all summer - one of the few annual plants that will. The daisy-like flowers add a mass of yellow to any arrangement.

Care: Very easy. Plant with slow-release fertilizer described on page 46, and leave them alone!

Water: Medium

Season: Summer. It does not like temperatures lower than 50 degrees.

Light: Medium shade to full sun

Zone: Use as an annual

Pest problems: Occasional fungus

Use: Mounding plant for sides and edges.

Size: 12 to 18 inches tall by equally as wide.

Colors: Yellow

Average life: 5 to 6 months

Cautions: Unknown

Red ribbon plants are defined on pages 18-19.

Plant Profiles: The High Performers

Mint, Variegated *(Plectranthus coleoides 'Variegata')*

Variegated mint is a fabulous plant. It trails well, lasts a long time, and requires nothing but water! I've had it in containers for six months and it looks like it's just getting started!

Care: Very easy. Plant with slow-release fertilizer described on page 46, and leave them alone!

Water: Medium

Season: Any frost-free season

Light: Medium shade to full sun in cool weather (under 85 degrees). Medium to light shade in hot weather (over 85 degrees).

Zone: Use as an annual.

Pest problems: Whiteflies

Use: Trailing or mounding plant. Good for sides and edges. Takes it a while to get started trailing down the sides. Does quite well planted through the side holes of a side-planted container.

Size: Trails 36 inches over the edge of a pot - eventually.

Colors: Light green and white

Average life: 6 months

Cautions: Unknown

Mona Lavender *(Plectranthus plepalila 'Mona Lavender')*

Mona Lavender did well in our container trials in cool weather but it doesn't flower in hot summers. It required no maintenance at all once it was planted, other than watering.

Care: Very easy. Plant with slow-release fertilizer described on page 46, and leave them alone!

Water: Medium

Season: Thrives in temperatures from 36 to 80 degrees.

Light: Medium shade to full sun in cooler weather, but burns in the summer sun.

Zone: Use as an annual.

Pest problems: None known

Use: Centerpiece or accent

Size: 16 to 18 inches tall with about the same spread.

Colors: Light, purple, spiky flowers; dark green leaves with solid purple undersides.

Average life: 6 months, but it only bloomed for a 3 month period, which is why it misses a ribbon.

Cautions: Unknown

Pansies *(Viola spp.)*

Pansies are just great for cool weather containers, where you can see the detail of those wonderful faces you often miss when they're planted in the garden. They are extremely easy to grow.

Care: Very easy. Plant with slow-release fertilizer described on page 46, and leave them alone!

Water: Medium. Water less in cooler weather, but don't let them go into a dry, cool spell with dry potting mix.

Season: Prefer temperatures from 20 degrees to 80 degrees. Don't look great at 20 degrees, but recover quickly when it warms up.

Light: Light shade to full sun

Zone: Different varieties have different cold tolerance.

Pest problems: Occasional slugs or aphids.

Use: Mounding plants for sides and edges. Does quite well planted through the side holes of a side-planted container.

Size: 4 to 6 inches tall by about 6 inches wide.

Colors: White, yellow, purple, brown, blue, pink, red, and multicolors.

Average life: 4 to 6 months in containers.

Cautions: Unknown

 Blue ribbon plants are defined on pages 14-15.

Pentas *(Pentas lanceolata)*

Pentas bloom for most of the summer, but don't rate a ribbon because many of the ones commonly sold now periodically go out of bloom. They are great for butterflies.

Care: Plant with slow-release fertilizer described on page 46, and leave them alone! Plants bloom more if you remove the dead flowers.

Water: Medium

Season: Any frost-free season. Takes high temperatures well.

Light: Light shade to full sun

Zone: Grown all over the world as a summer annual. Frost sensitive.

Pest problems: Mites

Use: Centerpiece or accent

Size: 12 to 18 inches tall in containers

Colors: Red, white, purple, or pink

Average life: 3 to 5 months

Cautions: Unknown

Note: I had consistent good luck with the older varieties of pentas. They never went out of bloom.

Some of the newer varieties are so dense they trap moisture and die quickly from fungus.

2ND Perilla *(Perilla frutescens 'Magilla')*

Perilla is quite similar to coleus. It misses a blue ribbon because it looks better with monthly trimming. Other than that, this is one, easy plant!

Care: Very easy. Plant with slow-release fertilizer described on page 46, and leave them alone! Trim to keep it from getting leggy.

Water: Medium

Season: Plant when temperatures vary between 40 degrees and the low-100's.

Light: Medium shade to full sun. Does better with a break from noon sun if the temperatures are over 90 degrees.

Zone: Use as an annual.

Pest problems: None known

Use: Centerpiece or accent. Does well in the sides of side-planted containers, staying quite compact.

Size: In the top of a large (17" D) container, has grown 4 feet tall in about 6 months. Stays shorter in smaller pots.

Colors: Burgundy leaves with hot pink centers.

Average life: At least 6 months

Cautions: Poisonous if eaten

1ST Persian Shield *(Strobilanthus dyeranus)*

Persian shield is a spectacular container plant. The leaves are so gorgeous they almost look artificial. They require nothing but water for a single season's use.

Care: Very easy. Plant with slow-release fertilizer described on page 46, and leave them alone!

Water: Medium

Season: Does best in temperatures from 40 degrees to the mid-90's.

Light: Medium shade to full sun in the cooler weather; light to medium shade in temperatures over the low-90's

Zone: Use as an annual.

Pest problems: None known

Use: Centerpiece or accent; didn't work well in the sides of side-planted baskets.

Size: In the top of a container, grows about 18 inches tall by 16 inches wide.

Colors: Purple

Average life: A year if protected from frost.

Cautions: Unknown

Red ribbon plants are defined on pages 18-19.

Plant Profiles: The High Performers

Petunia *(Petunia spp.)*

Petunias are one of the most popular container plants in the world. However, many of the unnamed varieties are quite short lived, so they don't rate a ribbon.

Care: Plant with slow-release fertilizer described on page 46. Remove the dead blooms if you have time.

Water: Medium

Season: Different varieties take different temperatures. None take freezing weather.

Light: Light shade to full sun

Zone: Use as an annual. Tolerant of light frost but not a freeze.

Pest problems: Fungus and whiteflies

Use: Mounding or trailing plant that works well along the edges. Tricky on the sides.

Size: All stay quite low, about 6 inches tall. Trailing varieties vary in spread, up to 3 feet.

Colors: Red, purples, white, yellow, or pink.

Average life: 1 to 6 months

Cautions: Unknown

1ST Phormium or Flax *(Aloe spp.)*

Flax is the epitome of a blue ribbon plant. Do absolutely nothing to it all season long! Great form and color for a centerpiece.

Care: Very easy. Plant with slow-release fertilizer described on page 46, and leave them alone!

Water: Low, but adapts to more water if planted with more thirsty plants.

Season: Plant when temperatures vary between 32 degrees and the low-100's.

Light: Light shade to full sun

Zone: Dies back to the ground in a freeze. Comes back in zones 8-10.

Pest problems: None known

Use: Centerpiece or accent

Size: About 2 feet tall in a container

Colors: Green, white, pink striped leaves.

Average life: 10 years

Cautions: Unknown

1ST Pothos *(Epipremnum aureum)*

Pothos is a workhorse houseplant. It survives more neglect than possibly any other indoor plant. It is quite useful outdoors, particularly in deep shade, where not too many plants grow.

Care: Very easy. Plant with slow-release fertilizer described on page 46, and leave them alone! Fertilize again in 6 to 9 months.

Water: Medium

Season: Protect from frost. Takes heat very well.

Light: Dense, medium, or light shade

Zone: 10b to 11. Tolerant of light frost but not a freeze.

Pest problems: None known

Use: Trailing plant. Does quite well planted through the side holes of a side-planted container.

Size: There may not be any limit as to the lengths their runners will grow. They can spread over an entire window ledge. The leaves grow much larger if the vine grows up instead of down.

Colors: Green and variegated

Average life: Years!

Cautions: Poisonous. Invasive in subtropical areas.

 Blue ribbon plants are defined on pages 14-15.

Salvia, annual *(Salvia spp.)*

1ST

Annual salvias are some of the most useful centerpiece plants for containers. They not only bloom for five to six months without stopping but also offer spiky flowers that contrast well with round ones.

Care: Very easy. Plant with slow-release fertilizer described on page 46, and leave them alone!

Water: Medium

Season: Any frost-free season. Requires more maintenance in hot temperatures. The dead blooms need to be removed.

Light: Light shade to full sun

Zone: Use as an annual.

Pest problems: I have never seen a pest on these plants but have heard of occasional thrips, mites, caterpillars, and slugs.

Use: Centerpiece or accent

Size: In the top of a container, the blue grows 15 to 18 inches tall. The red grows about 8 to 12 inches tall.

Colors: Many shades of white, red, peach, and purple.

Average life: 5 to 6 months

Cautions: Unknown

Salvia, 'Mystic Spires' *(Salvia 'Mystic Spires')*

1ST

Salvia 'Mystic Spires' is the best blue salvia I have found for containers. It grows compactly and doesn't fall over like some of the perennial blue salvias.

Care: Very easy. Plant with slow-release fertilizer described on page 46, and leave them alone! Remove dead flowers if you have the time.

Water: Medium

Season: Plant when temperatures vary between 32 degrees and the low-100's.

Light: Light shade to full sun

Zone: Use as an annual

Pest problems: None known

Use: Centerpiece or accent

Size: 12 to 18 inches tall

Colors: Blue

Average life: 6 months

Cautions: Unknown

Scaevola *(Scaevola spp.)*

1ST

Scaevola blooms non-stop in temperatures from 45 to the low-100's. And it lives for at least seven months with no care other than water!

Care: Very easy. Plant with slow-release fertilizer described on page 46, and leave them alone!

Water: Low

Season: Plant when temperatures vary between 45 degrees and the low-100's.

Light: Light shade to full sun

Zone: Use as an annual.

Pest problems: None known

Use: Trailing plant. Does quite well planted through the side holes of a side-planted container.

Size: Trails up to 36 inches down the sides of a container.

Colors: White or blue

Average life: 6 to 7 months

Cautions: Unknown

Red ribbon plants are defined on pages 18-19.

Plant Profiles: The High Performers

Sedum 'Angelina' *(Sedum spp.)*

Care: Very easy. Plant with slow-release fertilizer described on page 46, and leave them alone!

Water: Low, but adapts to more water if planted with more thirsty plants.

Season: Plant when temperatures vary between 32 degrees and the low-100's.

Light: Light shade to full sun

Zone: 3 to 11

Pest problems: I've never encountered any, but I've heard of occasional aphids.

Use: Mounding plant

Size: About 3 inches tall by 6 to 8 inches wide.

Colors: Lime green

Average life: 6 months as a decorative container plant because it dies back in cold temperatures.

Cautions: Unknown

Sedum 'Angelina' is the plant I use whenever I am stumped over what to put in a pot. When I get down to the final touches and need just one more plant, sedum always works.

Sempervivens *(Aloe spp.)*

Care: Very easy. Plant with slow-release fertilizer described on page 46, and leave them alone!

Water: Low

Season: Varies by type. Some are frost hardy and others aren't.

Light: Light shade to full sun

Zone: Varies by type

Pest problems: None known

Use: Some mound while others trail over the edge of a pot.

Size: Varies by type, but most are quite small.

Colors: Green, brown, red, maroons

Average life: 2 to 10 years

Cautions: Unknown

Sempervivens are succulents that are really easy to grow. Some are cold hardy. They come in many sizes and shapes, including rosette forms that resemble echeverias.

Shrimp Plant, Golden *(Pachystachys lutea)*

Care: Very easy. Plant with slow-release fertilizer described on page 46, and leave them alone! Looks better if you remove the dead flowers.

Water: Medium

Season: Any frost-free season. Takes high temperatures beautifully.

Light: Medium shade to full sun. Happier with some break from noon sun in summer.

Zone: 9 to 11. Use as an annual in other areas.

Pest problems: Caterpillars and snails

Use: Centerpiece or accent

Size: 1 to 2 feet tall

Colors: Yellow

Average life: 5 to 10 years in the ground in frost-free ares. 6 months in a container.

Cautions: Be sure to buy plants in bloom.

Golden shrimp plants dependably bloom all the time for months on end, which is perfect for containers. The spiky shape of the flowers is also an excellent textural addition to many arrangements.

 Blue ribbon plants are defined on pages 14-15.

Snapdragons *(Antirrhimum majus)*

Snapdragons are one plant I didn't like as well in containers as I do in the ground because they went out of bloom on me. The tall ones are gorgeous in containers, however.

Care: Plant with slow-release fertilizer described on page 46. Remove the dead flowers from the tall varieties.

Water: Medium

Season: Plant when temperatures vary between 32 degrees and the low-80's.

Light: Light shade to full sun

Zone: Summer annual in cooler areas of the world. Winter annual in south and central Florida. Tolerant of light frost but not freeze.

Pest problems: None known

Use: Centerpiece or accent

Size: In the top of a container, the tall ones grow to 36 inches tall. The dwarf variety grows to 6 inches tall.

Colors: Red, white, purple, orange, pink, salmon, and yellow.

Average life: 2 to 3 months as a decorative plant in a container.

Cautions: Unknown

Sweet Potato *(Ipomoea batatas)*

Sweet Potatoes are definitely the fastest growing trailing plant we have in this book, which can be a pain when they grow so fast they overtake other plants in the arrangement.

Care: Plant with slow-release fertilizer described on page 46, and leave them alone! Trim monthly or it will completely take over the container.

Water: Medium

Season: Plant when temperatures vary between 45 degrees and the low-100's.

Light: Medium shade to full sun

Zone: Use as an annual.

Pest problems: Snails, snails, and more snails! Japanese beetle attacks! Fungus, aphids, and white flies occasionally. I

have given up on trying to spray this plant and just put up with small holes in the leaves. I spray only when something is completely devouring it.

Use: Trailing plant

Size: They know no bounds...literally they'll shoot out ten feet!

Colors: Lime green, purplish-black, and pink.

Average life: 2 to 10 years

Cautions: Unknown

Note: The 'Sweet Caroline' variety is much more compact.

Syngonium, Nephthytis *(Syngonium spp.)*

Syngonium has been commonly used as a houseplant for generations. It is easy to grow and many new types are introduced each year. I use it in shady areas outside in summer.

Care: Very easy. Plant with slow-release fertilizer described on page 46, and leave them alone!

Water: Medium

Season: Plant when temperatures vary between 45 degrees and the low-100's.

Light: Dense, medium, or light shade

Zone: 10b to 11. Protect from frost.

Pest problems: Few problems outdoors. Scale, mealy bugs, aphids, and spider mites can be problems indoors.

Use: Trailing plant. Does quite well planted through the side holes of a side-planted container.

Size: Will trail several feet down the side of a container, but it takes quite a while.

Colors: Pink, peach, orange, red, and white.

Average life: Years in the same container if it is protected from frost.

Cautions: Invasive in the landscape. Contact with sap can cause pain and swelling.

Red ribbon plants are defined on pages 18-19.

Plant Profiles: The High Performers

Ti Plant *(Cordyline fructicosa)*

Ti Plants are one of the most useful centerpiece plants for container gardens. Their upright, spiky form contrasts well with round leaves and flowers. And they are simple to grow.

Care: Very easy. Plant with slow-release fertilizer described on page 46, and leave them alone! Fertilize again in 6 to 9 months.

Water: Medium

Season: Any frost-free season. (See 'Zone').

Light: Medium shade to full sun, depending on variety.

Zone: For most ti plants, use as an annual unless you live in a frost-free area. Some ti plants take temperatures down to the mid-20's.

Pest problems: If holes appear in the leaves, it is probably snails. I don't put out any snail bait unless the damage is extensive.

Use: Centerpiece or accent

Size: Varies by type. Most grow to about 2 feet tall in a typical container.

Colors: Shades of red, pink, and green

Average life: 6 months

Cautions: Unknown

Torenia, Trailing *(Torenia fournieri)*

Trailing torenias are one of the top performers from our container trials. They are not only very easy to grow but also bloom all year in frost-free areas, even in the hottest parts of summer.

Care: Very easy. Plant with slow-release fertilizer described on page 46, and leave them alone! Fertilize again in 6 to 9 months.

Water: Medium

Season: Any frost-free season

Light: Light shade to full sun

Zone: Tolerant of light frost but not a freeze.

Pest problems: None known

Use: Trailing plant for edges and sides

Does quite well planted through the side holes of a side-planted container.

Size: Grows about 6 to 12 inches down the side of a container.

Colors: Shades of blue, purple, and red

Average life: Up to one year with no frost.

Cautions: Unknown

Torenia, Upright *(Torenia fournieri)*

Torenias did well in our trials except they didn't last that long. They did great in the sides of the baskets, looking fabulous on planting day. However, they did disappear after two months or so.

Care: Plant with slow-release fertilizer described on page 46, and leave them alone!

Water: Medium

Season: Plant when temperatures vary between 50 degrees and the low-100's.

Light: Light shade to full sun

Zone: Summer annual in many parts of the world. Won't tolerate temperatures below 50 degrees.

Pest problems: Powdery mildew

Use: Mounding plant that works well alone or mixed with other bright colors. Works very well in sides of baskets.

Size: Mounds to about 8 inches tall and equally as wide.

Colors: Blue, pink, purple, white, red and multi. All have yellow centers.

Average life: 2 months in containers; 3 to 4 months in the landscape.

Cautions: Unknown

Blue ribbon plants are defined on pages 14-15.

Vinca Illumination *(Vinca 'Illumination')*

This vinca is an excellent long trailer that lasts a whole season with no care other than water! Use it with darker colors, like purple coleus, for contrast.

Care: Very easy. Plant with slow-release fertilizer described on page 46, and leave them alone!

Water: Medium

Season: Plant when temperatures vary between 45 degrees and the low-100's.

Light: Light shade to full sun

Zone: Use as an annual.

Pest problems: None known

Use: Trailing plant. Does quite well planted through the side holes of a side-planted container.

Size: Trails down about 3 feet

Colors: Yellow and green

Average life: 6 months

Cautions: Unknown

Vinca Vine *(Vinca major)*

Vinca vine is a container classic that has been considered a high performer for generations. It is a great choice for shade.

Care: Very easy. Plant with slow-release fertilizer described on page 46, and leave them alone!

Water: Medium

Season: Plant when temperatures vary between 45 degrees and the low-100's.

Light: Light to medium shade

Zone: Use as an annual

Pest problems: None known

Use: Trailing plant. Does quite well planted through the side holes of a side-planted container.

Size: Trails up to 6 feet down from the edge of a container.

Colors: Variegated green and white leaves.

Average life: About 6 months

Cautions: Unknown

Violas *(Viola spp.)*

Violas are similar to pansies except the flowers are smaller. They do well during the cool times of the year and thrive in shade.

Care: Very easy. Plant with slow-release fertilizer described on page 46, and leave them alone!

Water: Medium

Season: Plant when temperatures vary between 22 degrees and the low-80's.

Light: Medium shade to full sun

Zone: Use as an annual.

Pest problems: Occasional aphids or snails.

Use: Mounding plant that works well in the center or along the edges of any pot as well as in the sides of hanging baskets.

Size: 4 to 6 inches tall and equally as wide.

Colors: Lavender, blue, purple, red, brown, and yellow.

Average life: Grow for at least 6 months in zones 7 and 8 in winter. Shorter lifespan farther south. Do well for about 3 months in spring in zones 3 - 6. Bloom for most of the time they are alive.

Cautions: Unknown

Red ribbon plants are defined on pages 18-19.

Other Plants That Deserve Mention: *Notes from our ongoing trials*

Ageratum houstonianum
Ageratum
This annual is primarily useful for its interesting texture and pretty color. It stopped blooming periodically, taking rests for brief periods. Prefers sun. Lives for about three months.

Lobularia maritima
Alyssum
This cool-weather plant looks great along the edge, but not on the sides of instant containers. Grow it in full sun in temperatures that range from 36 to 85 degrees. Blooms for about three months.

Begonia spp.
Begonia, Cherry Blossom
A double wax begonia that is fabulous! Blooms a full 6 months in light to medium shade. Low water. Almost impossible to kill! Annual.

Begonia rex-cultorum
Begonia, Rex
Used for their striking leaf patterns in shade. Haven't lasted as long as other begonias in my trials.

Begonia tuberoso
Begonia, Tuberous
I have seen these doing beautifully in areas that have cool, dry summers. They have not done well in my trials, but I have never lived in a place with such a climate!

Ajuga repens 'Black Scallop'
Black Scallop
A perennial that does well in containers for at least 4 months in hot to cool weather. However, it stays quite small, so use it with plants that won't outgrow it. Medium shade to sun.

Iresine 'Blazin Rose'
Bloodleaf
Gorgeous leaves in this mounding plant that did fairly well but only lived for 3 months in containers.

Evolvulus glomeratus
Blue Daze
I used this plant a lot in containers until I discovered trailing torenia, which performs much better. Warm weather plant, but it stops blooming from time to time. Light shade to full sun. Lives about 6 months.

Bougainvillea spp.
Bougainvillea
A tropical that is commonly used as a patio plant in temperate areas. A little tricky. Blooms sporadically. Keep it on the dry side. Don't try it in heat over 95 degrees if you want blooms.

Celosia spp.
Celosia
I've had mixed results with these spiky plants. Some have lasted 6 months, while others have struggled to make it 2 months. Use as an annual.

Cleome hasslerana
Cleome
Summer annual that reseeds freely. Off and on bloomer, which makes it just ok for containers.

Cosmos spp.
Cosmos
Summer annual that reseeds freely. Gorgeous flowers, but the plants don't stay in bloom continuously for the whole season. Lasts about 3 months.

166 EASY CONTAINER GARDENS

Blue ribbon plants are defined on pages 14-15.

Curcuma 'Purple Prince'
Curcuma 'Purple Prince'
Glamorous, tropical plant that loves summer heat and grows 12" to 18" tall in a container, blooming for 1 to 2 months. Dormant (no leaves!) in winter. Zones 10 to 11 or protect from frost.

Osteospermum spp.
Daisy, Cape
This daisy only bloomed for about a month in our trials. I don't know if it blooms longer in other parts of the world.

Thymophylla tenuiloba
Daisy, Dahlberg
These are still mysterious to me - some years they've thrived and others, not done so well. I love the little flowers, but they just live for a few months.

Ageranthemum houstonianum
Daisy, Marguerite
This popular plant has a flower that is larger than the longer-blooming California daisy. Did well for us in cooler, spring temperatures, but not in heat over 93 degrees. Bloomed for about 3 months.

Delphinium spp.
Delphinium
This plant is grown both as an annual and perennial. Many different types are available. I only tried the one shown above. It did quite well in full sun and cool (40 to 70 degree) temperatures, but only for 3 months.

Dianthus spp.
Dianthus
Many professionals swear by dianthus, but I haven't found any great ones yet. I use them in containers for their showy flowers, knowing they will bloom for a month, go out of bloom, and resume in another month or two.

Diascia spp.
Diascia
We were quite impressed by the Diascia 'Miracle' we tested from Bodger Botanicals (through Michell's). It bloomed quite well in temperatures ranging from 45 to 90 degrees for a full, six months.

Cineria spp.
Dusty Miller
An excellent annual - easy and dependable. Doesn't do well in the sides of side-planted containers, but thrives along the edges. Use in full sun in cooler temperatures.

Euphorbia 'Diamond Frost'
Euphorbia 'Diamond Frost'
I have had only one season's experience with this wildly popular plant. It did quite well, but only lasted about 3 months. I will definitely try this one again.

Selaginella uncinata
Fern, Blue Peacock or Moss, Peacock Spike
Very useful filler for pots. Grows quickly. Quite low in form. Best in light to medium shade. Zones 9b to 11. Use as summer annual in other zones.

Fuchsia spp.
Fuchsia
So many varieties! Some like it cold, and others like it hot. Some bloom briefly, and others for months. If you see one you like, ask the garden center staff if it will perform the way you need it to.

Gerbera jamesonii
Gerber Daisy
Lovely but very short-lived plant. Only lives and blooms for about a month.

Other Plants That Deserve Mention: *Notes from our ongoing trials*

Pennisetum 'Red Riding Hood'
Grass, 'Red Riding Hood'
Excellent centerpiece plant that lasted all season and even took frost without dying back! About 18 inches tall and spreading.

Heliotropum peruvianum
Heliotrope
I've seen this plant doing beautifully in areas with cool summers, like parts of California and Vancouver. I have not had consistent luck with it yet, but that could be because the temperatures in my garden are too hot.

Hibiscus spp.
Hibiscus
Tropical plant that is used throughout the world as a summer patio plant. Blooms intermittently. Flowers stick to pavement. Full sun to light shade. Many sizes and colors available. Over winters well indoors.

Helichrysum thianschanicum
Icicles
A filler plant that did quite well in our cool weather trials. We didn't try it in the heat of summer. Grows to about 5" tall in a container. Use as an annual in Florida. Prefers light shade.

Impatiens 'Little Lizzie'
Impatiens 'Little Lizzie'
A dwarf variety that deserves much more use in containers. Thrives both along the edges and in the sides of instant containers. Lasts 6 months, blooming continuously.

Alternanthera spp.
Jacob's Coat
An excellent annual - easy and dependable in the ground as long as it's not too wet. Doesn't do well in the sides of instant containers. Quite small, so use slow-growing plants around it. Lives about 3 months in containers.

Jatropha spp.
Jatropha
A wonderful tropical shrub that deserves more use in temperate areas as a summer annual. Blooms continuously in temperatures from 45 to 95 degrees for many years if protected from frost.

Kalanchoe blossfeldiana
Kalanchoe
Beautiful flowers that bloom in sun or shade. Succulent. Very erratic bloom period. I've seen it bloom for one month and stop and I've also seen it bloom for 4 months straight.

Liriope spp.
Liriope, Monkey Grass
A tried-and-true plant for most areas of the world. Takes sun or shade. Works well as a centerpiece provided the edge plants don't grow taller than the liriope. Easily lasts a full season.

Lobelia spp.
Lobelia
One of my favorite container plants that has not been dependable in the sides of side-planted containers. Prefers cooler temperatures. I need to do a lot more work on this one!

Calibrachoa x hybridus
Million Bells, Calibrachoa
I have had erratic results with this plant. Some have done quite well while others die quickly. I still have a lot more varieties to test. Plant in sun and protect from freezes.

Portulaca grandiflora
Moss Rose
Although this tough plant requires little water, I don't like it in containers because it only blooms for short periods during each day when it is hot.

 Blue ribbon plants are defined on pages 14-15.

Catharanthus roseus
Periwinkle

I have had a lot of fungus problems with periwinkle in containers. But, they thrive in the ground in areas with low to medium rainfall.

Phlox spp.
Phlox

There are both annual and perennial forms of this plant. I tested the annuals in containers. They were gorgeous, but bloomed intermittently and didn't last the whole season.

Plumbago auriculata
Plumbago

Plumbago is a great perennial in the ground in zones 9 to 11. It is not my favorite container plant, however, because of its sporadic bloom cycle.

Hypoestes phyllostachya
Polka Dot Plant

I tested this one because of its reputation for taking deep shade. It did alright, but not particularly well. In deep shade, it became leggy quickly.

Tradescantia pallida 'Purpurea'
Purple Queen

Purple queen grows incredibly well in containers. It sticks out awkwardly, however, and I haven't yet found companion plants to mask this weird growth habit.

Portulaca oleracea
Purslane

Although this tough plant requires little water, I don't like it in containers because it only blooms for short periods during each day when it is hot.

Fittonia verschaffeltii
Red Ann Fittonia

I found this plant in the houseplant section of a garden center. It takes medium to light shade, grows to about 6" tall, and lives for about 6 months in a container. Protect from frost.

Schizanthus pinnatus
Schizanthus, Poor Man's Orchid

I really enjoyed working with this beautiful plant. It only lasted a month or two as an edge plant, but its label prepared me for its short life. Likes cool temperatures.

Senecio radicans
String of Bananas

Interesting, easy succulent that trails down the sides of containers. Very low water.

Verbena spp.
Verbena

Upright verbena died quickly in the sides of my containers. Trailing verbena did much better, but didn't bloom consistently or last through an entire, 6 month season. Prefers sun and warm temperatures.

Zinnia spp.
Zinnia

An excellent centerpiece plant for hot temperatures if you can find one that doesn't come down with fungus! Likes sun.

Bibliography

Armitage, Allan. *Armitage's Garden Annuals*. Portland, Oregon: Timber Press, 2004.

Baldwin, Debra Lee. *Designing with Succulents*. Timber Press, 2007.

Cave, Yvonne. *Succulents*. Portland, Oregon: Timber Press, 2002.

Crawford, Pamela. *Container Gardens for Florida*. Canton, Georgia: Color Garden Publishing. 2005.

Crawford, Pamela. *Instant Container Gardens*. Canton, Georgia: Color Garden Publishing. 2007.

Morton, Julia. *Plants Poisonous to People*. Miami, Florida: Hallmark Press. 1995.

Ross, Susan, and Schrader, Dennis. *Hot Plants for Cool Climates*. New York: Houghton Mifflin Company, 2000.

Smith, P. Allen. *Container Gardens*. New York, New York: Clarkson Potter/Publishers, 2005.

Williams, Paul. *Container Gardening*. New York, New York: DK Publishing, 2004.

Index

Dicondra 'Silver Falls' at Longwood Gardens in Kennett Square, Pennsylvania.